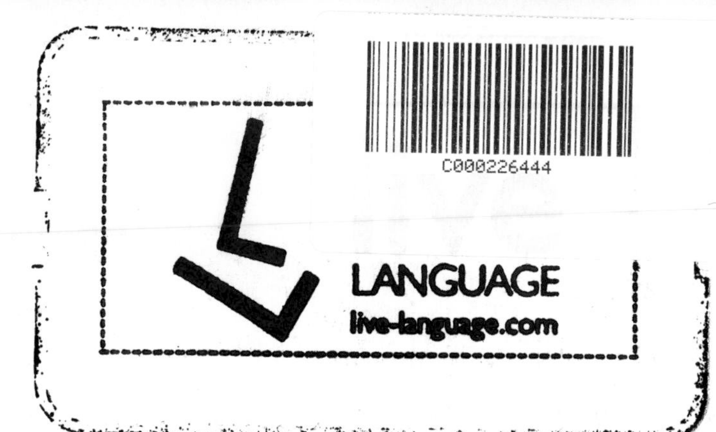

ADVENTURES

Student's Book

Intermediate

Ben Wetz
and Mick Gammidge

Reading and Listening	Speaking	Writing	Pronunciation and Study skills
• Memories • Time • Captain Cook • Name the date	• Talking about periods in history • Talking about when you were younger	• Expressing opinion: *I think / don't think that... in my opinion... for me...*	• *used (to)*
• Attraction • Couples • From the heart	• Survey • Asking and answering about recent activities	• Giving reasons: *so, so that, that's why* and *because*	• Weak forms • Using a dictionary (1): checking pronunciation
• Teenagers • The Story of Pop: Rock	• Inviting someone	• Project: make a poster	
• Charity • Debate • A good cause	• Listing priorities	• Planning your writing	• *-tion* • Using a dictionary (2): finding the best definition
• A new look • Appearances • Fashion victims	• Talking about people • Winning the lottery • Discussing appearances • Completing a questionnaire	• A report: presenting statistics	• Silent consonants
• Teenagers and the law • The Story of Pop: Punk	• Ordering in a café	• Project: making a poster	
• Masterpieces • Art or crime • Reaction	• Giving opinions about art • Talking about an art crime • Talking about modern art	• A biography: editing a text	• Recognizing contractions
• Express yourself • Habits • Emotions	• Describing body language and personality • Completing a questionnaire	• Revision of linking words and phrases	• Moving stress • Learning vocabulary: adjectives and nouns
• On the road • The Story of Pop: Hip hop	• Asking for and giving permission	• Project: making a leaflet	• Rhythm and intonation
• Hotels • Around the world • Travelling companions	• Talking about geography • Travel • Finding a good travel companion	• An informal letter	• *the* • Checking your written work
• Prize money • Computer games • Television	• Talking about TV likes and dislikes • Discussing good and bad things about TV	• A 'for and against' composition	• Word stress: number of syllables
• Teenage magazines • The Story of Pop: Latin music	• Asking for and giving advice	• Project: designing a magazine	
• Animal talk • Message and meaning • Get the message	• Identifying reporting verbs • Ask and answer a questionnaire	• Designing a questionnaire	• Intonation in question tags • Making vocabulary notes
• The guardian • The unexplained • UFO mania	• Telling a story • Making deductions about the past	• Using time connectors: *while, suddenly, at first, later* and *eventually*	
• Text messages • The Story of Pop: Dance	• Text messages	• Project: doing a survey and making a graph	

OXFORD
UNIVERSITY PRESS

Great Clarendon Street, Oxford OX2 6DP

Oxford University Press is a department of the University of Oxford. It furthers the University's objective of excellence in research, scholarship, and education by publishing worldwide in

Oxford New York

Auckland Cape Town Dar es Salaam Hong Kong Karachi Kuala Lumpur Madrid Melbourne Mexico City Nairobi New Delhi Shanghai Taipei Toronto

With offices in

Argentina Austria Brazil Chile Czech Republic France Greece Guatemala Hungary Italy Japan Poland Portugal Singapore South Korea Switzerland Thailand Turkey Ukraine Vietnam

OXFORD and OXFORD ENGLISH are registered trade marks of Oxford University Press in the UK and in certain other countries

First published 2005
2009 2008 2007 2006 2005
10 9 8 7 6 5 4 3 2 1

ISBN-13: 978 0 19 437663 1
ISBN-10: 0 19 437663 X

Printed in Spain by Just Colour Graphic, S. L.

ACKNOWLEDGEMENTS

The authors and publisher are grateful to those who have given permission to reproduce the following extracts and adaptations of copyright material: p 18 *Message in a Bottle*. Words and music by Sting. © 1979 G. M. Sumner. EMI Music Publishing Ltd / Magnetic Publishing Ltd. Reproduced by permission of Music Sales Ltd. All rights reserved. International copyright secured. p 26 *We Will Rock You*. Words and music by Brian May. © 1977 Queen Music Ltd. EMI Music Publishing Ltd, London WC2H 0EA. Reproduced by permission of International Music Publications Ltd. p 48 *I Fought the Law*. Words and music by Sonny Curtis. © 1961 (renewed 1989) Acuff-Rose Music Incorporated, USA. Acuff-Rose Music Limited, 25 James Street, London W1. Reproduced by permission of Music Sales Ltd. All Rights Reserved. International copyright secured. p 70 *It's like that*. Words and music by Larry Smith, Joseph Simmonds and Darryll McDaniels. © 1987 Rush Groove Music and Protoons Inc, USA. Warner/Chappell Music Ltd. London W6 8BS. Reproduced by permission of International Music Publications Ltd. p 74 'The first verified walk round the earch' by Dave Kunst. From www.Earthlink.net. Reproduced by permission of Dave Kunst, 1996 Olympic Torchbearer & Guiness Record Breaker. p 92 *Livin' la vida loca*. Words and music by Robi Rosa and Desmond Child. © 1999 A Phantom Vox Publishing and Desmophobia, USA. 50% Warner/Chappell Music Ltd. London W6 8BS. 50% Universal Music Publishing Ltd. Reproduced by permission of International Music Publications Ltd & Universal Music Publishing Ltd. p 104 Adapted from *The X-Files Book of the Unexplained* Volume I by Jane Goldman. Copyright © Jane Goldman, 1996 Twentieth Century Fox Corporation. All rights reserved. Published by Simon and Schuster UK Ltd. Reproduced by permission of Simon Schuster Ltd. p 114 *Praise You*. Words and Music by Cook & Yarbrough. © 1998. Reproduced by permission of Universal Music Publishing Ltd.

Art editing by: Pictureresearch.co.uk

Illustrations by: Emma Dodd pp 31 (politicians), 67, 76, 95, 100, 103, 108, 111; Mark Duffin pp 8, 71, 106 (Romans and War of the Worlds), 107; Roger Fereday pp 23, 42, 62, 89, 101; Sara Palma p 51; Andy Parker p 31 (cloned women); Louisa St Pierre pp 13, 102; Carol Seatory pp 12 (Sally), 16, 45, 83, 96; Martin Shovel pp 12, 39, 56, 59, 93, 105; Mike Stones p 12 (Babushka).

Commissioned Photography by: Emily Andersen pp 21 (Phil & Kim), 23, 43 (cafe), 45, 65 (mother & daughter), 67, 82 (boy playing game & Nintendo games); Steve Betts pp 9, 11, 15 (boy), 36 (image consultant), 50 (Jane's picture), 87 (boys and motorcyle & magazines), 89, 90 (magazines), 112; Chris King pp 7, 38, 57 (stare & sneer).

We would also like to thank the following for permission to reproduce the following photographs: Action Plus 98 (football/N.Tingle); Alamy pp 19 (BananaStock), 27 (Earth/Brand X Pictures), 28 (Fiona/image100 & Elaine/J.Smith), 36 (girl/ plainpicture), 57 (crying/f1online/F.Stenson), 61 (boy/Big Cheese Photo), 63 (girl/ Alexandra Carlile), 68 (speed camera /M.Sykes), (speed limit sign/thislife pictures), 69 (truck/f1online/M.Leder), (freeway/picturescolourlibrary.com), (30m.p.h./M.Hill), (Don't Walk/M.Del Grosso), 84 (J.Wiedel), 96 (David R.Frazier Photolibrary, Inc.), 100 (BananaStock); Allsport p 90 (footballer); The Andy Warhol Foundation Inc / Art Resource/New York p 54 (Andy Warhol Brillo Box); The Art Archive p 106 (medieval manuscript/Bibliothèque Municipale Valenciennes/Dagli Orti); Atari Historical Society www.atari-history.com 82 (Pong); The Bridgeman Art Library pp 49 (Gaugin: Women in Tahiti), (Velasquez: The Spinners), (Van Gogh: Starry Night over the Rhone), (Leonardo da Vinci: Mona Lisa), 50 (Velasquez: An Old Woman Cooking Eggs), 54 (Marcel Duchamp: Nude descending a staircase no 2, 1912, Philadelphia Museum of Art, Pennsylvania © DACS 2005), 56 (Popova Untitled 1916), (Goya: The Naked Maja), (Bloemers: Still Life with Fruit and Dead Partridge), (Goya: Self portrait aged 65), (Duchamp-Villon, The Horse, 1914), (Van Gogh: Landscape at Auvers after the Rain), (Van Gogh: Self-portrait); BBC Photograph Library pp 79 (soap), 79 (News); Bruce Coleman p 79 (panda/Hans Reinhard); Camera Press pp 26 (Freddy Mercury), 35 (geisha), 35 (face piercing/Martin Godwin), 72 (ice hotel /Peter Grant), 104 (Erika Zur Stinberg/Ralph Metzger), 104 (Uri Geller); Celador pp 79 (game show), 80 (*Who wants to be a Millionaire*); Channel 4 p 79 (chat show); Corbis pp 5 (dinosaur/L.Psihoyos), (spear,axe/ Archivo Iconografico, S.A.), (ruins/E.Ciol), (modern architecture/T.Bognár), (16th century dress/Historical Picture Archive), (knight/K.Fleming), (coach/ Hulton-Deutsch Collection), 25 (beach/C.Aurness), (radio/Westlight Stock/OZ Productions), (money/Westlight Stock/OZ Productions), 27 (rat/M.Beauregard), (cattle/A.Arbib), (terrorist/SYGMA), (beggar/V.Moos), (tank), 37 (shopping/ N.Schaefer), 58 (wolf), 73 (capsule hotel/R.Ressmeyer), 80 (Twenty-one), 94 (chimpanzee/A.Clopet), 98 (listening/T.Stewart), 106 (UFO 1954/Bettmann); Getty Images pp 6 (boy in tie), 10 (Colosseum), (yo-yo/Hulton Archive), 14 (woman/Thinkstock), 15 (couple with glass/Telegraph Colour Library), (couple with motor bike/A.Tilley), 20 (perfume), (flowers), (chain), (Priya), 21 (group of students/Taxi), 25 (students/Taxi), 28 (Barry/Photodisc Red/ E.May), 30 (Dr Nutall), (Tanner), 35 (woman and rings), 36 (boy/L.Bobbe), 37 (boy/S.Kushner), 40 (shoes), (crinoline/Hulton Archive), 42 (Colin), 44 (interview/Daly & Newton), 47 (wedding/R.Brimson), 47 (driver/Comstock Images), 57 (kissing), 57 (point/Altrendo Images), 58 (crying), 58 (kissing), 59 (smile /A.Wolfe), 59 (kissing/Frank Clarkson), 63 (boy/P.Cade), 68 (motor bike/Photodisc/K.Weatherly), 68 (racing bike /C.Cole), 73 (beach/A.Blomqvist), 79 (sport/M.Powell), 84 (family 1950s/Telegraph Colour Library), 84 (teenagers watching TV/Olivier Ribardiere), 91 (girl/R.Anania), 91 (boy/J.Chillingworth/ Hulton Archive), 94 (dolphin/J.Rotman), 108 (T.Flach); Phil Hankinson p 16; Damien Hurst / White Cube p 54 (Damien Hurst, *The Physical Impossibility of Death in the Mind of Someone Living*); David Kunst p 74; The Kobal Collection p 79 (drama); Last Resort p 68 (Driving License); London Features International pp 21 (Queen/Simon Fowler), 65 (Run DMC/Dennes Van Tine/ VDV/G9), 90 (Eminem/Ron Wolfson), 109 (Fat Boy Slim/David Fisher); Marley Davidson p 42 (Spike); Mary Evans Picture Library pp 10 (Captain Cook & Santa Maria), 40 (wig); Kate Mellersch / OUP p 52; Network Photographers p 28 (Aids/Laurie Sparham); Panos Pictures p 28 (bird/Chris Stowers); Powerstock / Zefa pp 42 (Stella), 57 (smiling), 64, 106 (cityscape); Redferns p 114 (clubbing/Simon King), (Fat Boy Slim/Tony Buckingham); Retna pp 70 (DMC performing/Tara Canova), 113 (red spot dress/Grayson Alexander), 113 (large group & three judges/Sara De Boer); Rex Features pp 5 (Beatles/ Everett Collection), 26 (Queen), 27 (inoculation/Phanie Agency), 35 (punk), (tattoo/Jim Jones), 42 (Dawn), 47 (voting/Sipa Press), 48, 53 (artist), 55, 68 (scooter /MB Pictures), 70 (DMC posed/B.Rasic), 72 (capsule hotel/Ben Simmons), 92 (Ricky Martin pointing/Brian Rasic); Royalty-free pp 6 (toddler), 14 (bottle),(couple),(rose), 18, 22, 24, 35 (clown), (surgery), 43 (driving), 53 (Sam), 57 (blushing), 58 (shaking hands/Stockbyte), 60, 61 (canoeing), 66, 68 (L plate), 88, 109 (woman), (texting), 110; Science Photo Library pp 27 (dna/P.Plailly/Eurelios), 44 (Earth), 72 (space hotel/Victor Habbik), 78 (Earth/Worldsat International), 98 (looking/ M. Fermariello); Frank Spooner Pictures/Corbis pp 28 (doctor/Turpin), 35 (eyes), 57 (shake hands), 72 (undersea lodge), 78 (Ffyonna Campbell/Stephen Lock), 79 (The Simpsons), 92 (Ricky Martin clapping/Turiak); Still Pictures p 32; The Stockmarket p 57 (hugging/A.Skelley); Tate Gallery, London p 49 (Picasso Weeping Woman/ © Succession Picasso/DACS 2005); Courtesy of Tiger Beat p 91; Tracey Emin/ White Cube p 54 (Tracy Emin My Bed); TRIP /Art Directors pp 53 (Eva), 59 (hug/Helene Rogers), 65 (motorbike); Zefa p 20 (ring & chocolates).

Days and dates

Have a look!

Find the pages where you:

- **listen to a history quiz.**
- **think about objects from a museum.**
- **read about young people's memories.**

Vocabulary

Periods: adjectives

1 **Match the words in the box with pictures 1–8. Then listen and check.**

> Victorian medieval prehistoric
> 15th-century ~~modern~~ 1960s
> Bronze-age ancient

8 modern

VOCABULARY PAGE 124, 1.1

Speaking

2 **Work in pairs.**

1. What happened in each period?
2. Which period would you like to have lived in?
3. Which period would you not like to have lived in?

1a Memories

Reading

1 Read and listen. Then answer the questions.

1 When did Holly go to France?
2 When did people laugh at Liam?

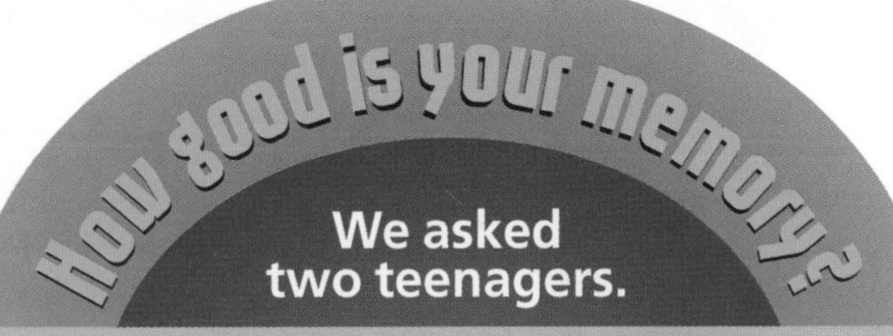

Holly

What do you remember?

Your earliest memory
I'm not sure, but I think I was two. I remember a holiday with my mum and dad. We stayed near a beach. Where were we? France, I think. I can see myself paddling in the sea and holding my father's hand.

Your first day at school
That was eleven years ago! It was awful. I just remember a lot of loud people. When Mum came for me after school, I was crying so hard she thought I was hurt.

Liam

Your earliest memory
I think I was three. I was feeding the ducks by the lake in the park when I fell in the water. I don't remember what happened next. It was a long time ago.

Your first day at school
While I was going to school, some people from another school laughed at my uniform. I hate it when people laugh at me. And I hated it even more when I was little. I was so self-conscious.

How do you remember important things?

Holly: I think my memory is OK, but it's not brilliant. I'm reading a good book at the moment. It's by a psychologist and it's about how to improve your memory. I'm using her suggestions and they're working. Her suggestions for remembering vocabulary in foreign languages really work. You just imagine the words you are learning as images. They could be things or actions or both. For example, if you are learning shopping items, you imagine a shop and where the items are. The *sugar* and *pasta* on the shelves and the *ham* and *cooked meat* in the fridge, and so on. When you want to remember a word, you enter the shop in your imagination and find the item and you should remember what it is called.

Liam: I make lots of lists. Each list starts off about ten items long, because that's the most I can remember in one go. To be honest, even that is sometimes too many. I repeat the list over and over until I think I remember it. Then I test myself after half an hour, then after half a day and after a day. After that, I try to revise the lists every few days. I'm studying for an exam at the moment and the method is helping for some things, but it is hard to remember everything. There are some things I just can't remember. I seem to have a mental block about important dates in history for example. Maybe it's because they were so long ago.

2 Read the text again. Are the sentences true or false?

1 Liam remembers when he was three years old.
2 Holly enjoyed her first day at school.
3 Liam thought his first day at school was funny.
4 Holly doesn't think that the book on memory is good.
5 Holly is learning about shops.
6 Liam cannot remember dates very well.

Look!
ago
It was a long time **ago**!
That was eleven years **ago**!

GRAMMAR PAGE 116

Exploring grammar

Present simple and present continuous

3 Match the rules with the examples.

Present simple

(1) ...... I make lots of lists.

Present continuous

(2) ...... I'm studying for an exam at the moment.

Rules

a We use this tense to talk about an action that is happening now.

b We use this tense to talk about routines and repeated actions or states.

GRAMMAR PAGE 115

4 Choose the correct form of the verbs.

1 Psychologists often **use** / **are using** memory tests.

2 These tests **find out** / **are finding out** how much we remember.

3 They **don't test** / **aren't testing** your general knowledge.

4 Holly **takes** / **is taking** a memory test at the moment.

5 She **answers** / **is answering** questions about the things she remembers.

6 She **doesn't do** / **isn't doing** very well.

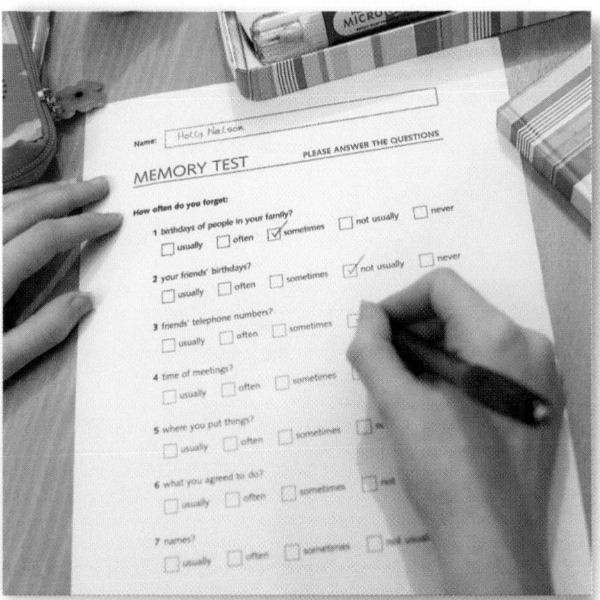

Past simple and past continuous

5 Look at the examples and complete the rule with the past simple and the past continuous.

When Mum **came** for me after school, I **was crying**.
I **was feeding** ducks when I **fell** in the water.

Rule

When we use the **past simple** and the **past continuous** together, we use the **past** ...... to talk about an action that happened in the middle of another, longer action. We use the **past** ...... for the longer action.

GRAMMAR PAGE 115

6 Write sentences. Use the past simple and the past continuous.

While Liam / wait / for his friends, / he / buy / a great T-shirt.

While Liam was waiting for his friends, he bought a great T-shirt.

1 Liam and his friends / watch / the film when his mobile phone / ring.

2 When he / talk / on the phone, / a woman / say, / 'Turn it off!'

3 While Holly and her friends / chat, / they / decide / to have a pizza.

4 While Holly / call / The Pizza Place, / her Dad / arrive / home with pizzas!

7 Complete the questions with the past simple and the past continuous. Then ask your partner.

MEMORY TEST

Where *did you go* last Saturday?

What **(1)** ..... (you / do) at 3 o'clock last Sunday?

What **(2)** ..... (you / study) when the last lesson **(3)** ..... (end)?

(4) ..... (you / dream) when you **(5)** ..... (wake up) this morning?

Finished?

Write about some of your memories.
My last birthday was good. I met some ...

1b Time

Vocabulary

Periods of time

1 Write the words in order of length of time. Then listen and check.

century decade hour millennium
minute month ~~second~~ week season
year day fortnight

VOCABULARY PAGE 124, 1.2

second

Listening

2 Guess what people used these objects for. Then listen to a museum guide and check.

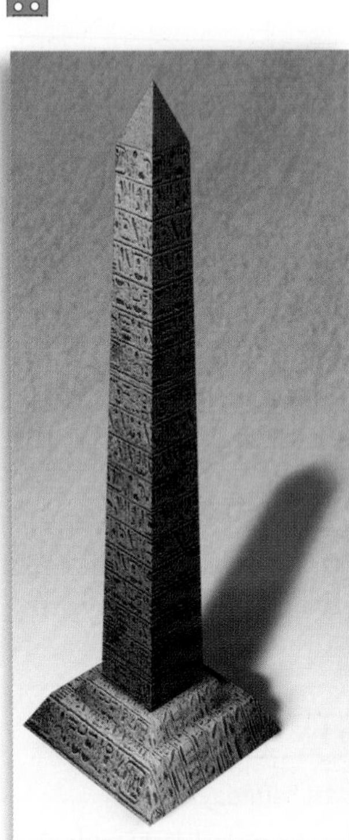

The Egyptians used obelisks as a

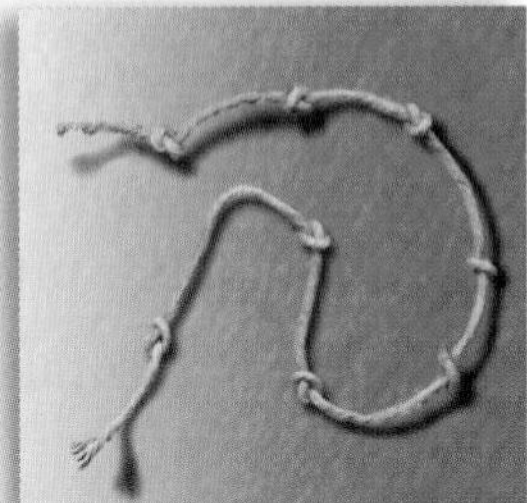

This string with knots in it was a way of

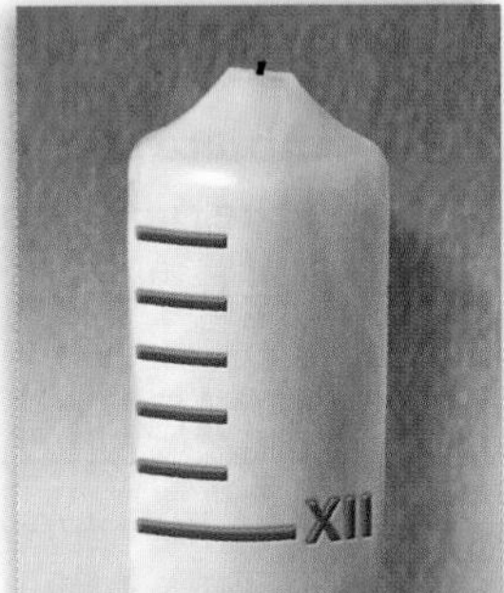

This is a special candle that people used to

People used this stick with lines cut in it to

This bowl with lines inside it is a

3 Listen to the museum guide again and answer the questions.

1. Why did the first clocks have only one hand?
2. Where were the first watches made?
3. Why didn't most people have watches in the 17th century?
4. Who were the first people to use water clocks?
5. When did the Egyptians begin to use obelisks as clocks?
6. How long ago did people start to count the days of the moon?

Exploring grammar

Past simple and past perfect

4 Look at the examples. Underline the first action in time in each sentence. Then complete the rules.

The Greeks **used** water clocks about 325 BC but the Egyptians **had had** them a millennium earlier.
People **had used** the sun for centuries before they **invented** water clocks.

Rules

When one action happens before another action, we use the **past** (1) ...... for the first action in time and the **past** (2) ...... for the second action in time.
To make the **past perfect**, we use **had** + (3) ....

GRAMMAR PAGES 115–116

IRREGULAR VERBS INSIDE FRONT COVER

5 Complete the dialogue. Use the past simple and the past perfect.

Jess: You didn't go on the school trip to London yesterday. Where were you?

Matt: I was late! The coach (**1**) ...... (leave) when I (**2**) ...... (arrive) at school.

Jess: Why were you late?

Matt: At my bus stop, I (**3**) ...... (realize) that I (**4**) ...... (forget) my money! I had to go home to get it. Was the trip fun?

Jess: Yes, it was. I (**5**) ...... (not visit) the Museum of Time before, so I (**6**) ..... (learn) a lot yesterday. It's really interesting.

Matt: I know. I often used to go there with my parents when we lived in London.

Jess: In London? When was that? I didn't know you lived there!

Matt: I (**7**) ...... (finish) primary school, so I think we (**8**) ..... (come) here when I was eleven.

used to

We use *used to* for regular actions in the past that don't happen now.

6 Study the rules and the examples. Complete the sentences using *used to*, *didn't use to* and the verb in brackets.

Affirmative

We use **used to + infinitive.**
Watches **used to be** very expensive. (be)
1 Watches ..... a lot of money. (cost)

Negative

We use **didn't use to + infinitive.**
Most people **didn't use to have** them. (have)
2 Poor people ..... them. (buy)

GRAMMAR PAGE 116

7 Write sentences with *used to* and *didn't use to*. Use the verbs in the box.

think ~~visit~~ not live not know go

Matt *used to visit* the museum with his parents.

1 His family ...... in Oxford.
2 Matt ...... to school in London.
3 Jess ...... that Matt was from Oxford.
4 She ...... a lot about the history of time.

Pronunciation

/ju:zd/ and /ju:st/

8 Listen and repeat. How is the pronunciation of *used* different?

1 I used the internet to find some information.
2 My parents used to use books before the internet.

9 Practise saying these sentences. Then listen and check.

1 We use clocks these days.
2 People didn't use to use clocks.
3 They used to use candles.

Speaking

10 Work in pairs. Ask and answer questions about when you were eight years old. Use the ideas in the box.

your free time your friends
your holidays your favourite places

A: What did you use to do in your free time when you were eight?

B: I used to collect ...

Finished?

Write about what you and your partner used to do when you were eight.

1c Name the Date

Reading

1 Read the text and complete the sentences.

Captain Cook

In 1770, Captain James Cook and his crew arrived in Australia. They were the first British people to visit it but not the first Europeans – a Dutchman called Abel Tasman first went to the north of Australia in 1642. Cook was on his first voyage round the world. His small ship, the *Endeavour*, which normally held a crew of seventeen, left England with 94 people on it. They included officers, crew and scientists. There were also two dogs and a goat for milk. Among the scientists on Cook's ship were botanists. They found so many new plants where they landed in Australia that they called it Botany Bay. The reason for the journey was to make maps and drawings of plants and animals, as well as to collect samples of some of the plants. Cook took the eastern coast of Australia for Britain, but at that time he didn't know just how big Australia was. This journey changed the nature of exploration. It was the start of journeys for scientific discovery and the start of Britain's relationship with Australia.

1 The first European to go to Australia was ....
2 Cook arrived in eastern Australia in .....
3 The *Endeavour* usually had .... people on board.
4 They called the place they landed Botany Bay because ....
5 The reason for the journey was to ....
6 Cook didn't know ....

Listening

2 Match events 1–3 with dates from a–f. Then listen and check.

a	72	d	33
b	1490	e	1492
c	1936	f	1986

1 The Romans built the Colosseum approximately two thousand years ago. They started it in the year ....

2 Columbus first explored in the Santa María in the year ....

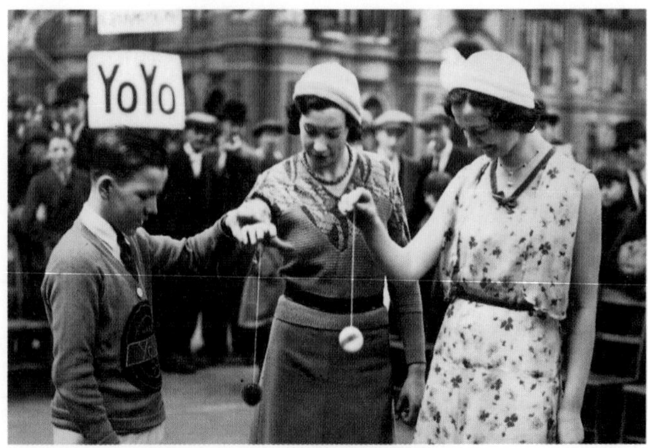

3 Yo-yos first became popular in the year ....

3 Listen again and answer these questions.

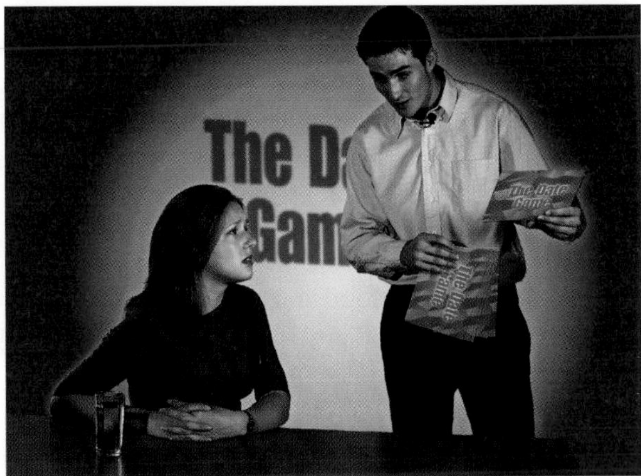

1 Did Avril feel nervous?
2 Did her parents go with her?
3 How much time did she have to answer each question?
4 How many questions did Avril answer?
5 Did she win a prize?

Writing

Expressing opinions: *I think / don't think that, in my opinion, for me*

4 Find the three expressions that Steve uses to give his opinions in the email below. Which expressions have commas after them?

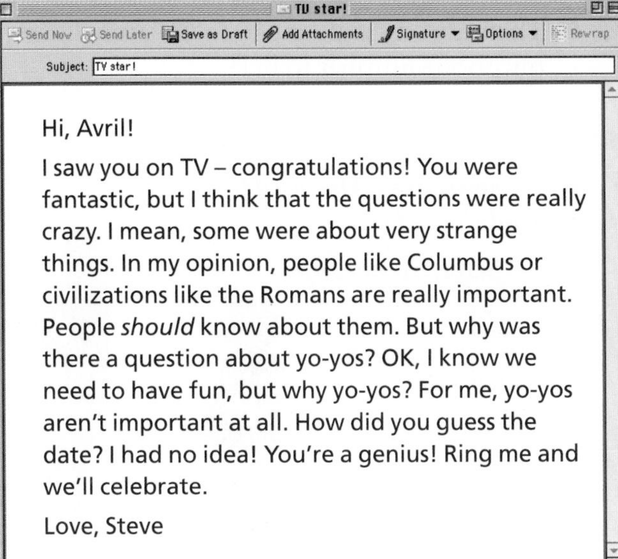

Hi, Avril!

I saw you on TV – congratulations! You were fantastic, but I think that the questions were really crazy. I mean, some were about very strange things. In my opinion, people like Columbus or civilizations like the Romans are really important. People *should* know about them. But why was there a question about yo-yos? OK, I know we need to have fun, but why yo-yos? For me, yo-yos aren't important at all. How did you guess the date? I had no idea! You're a genius! Ring me and we'll celebrate.

Love, Steve

5 Complete the text with the words from the box.

In ~~think that~~ for don't think opinion

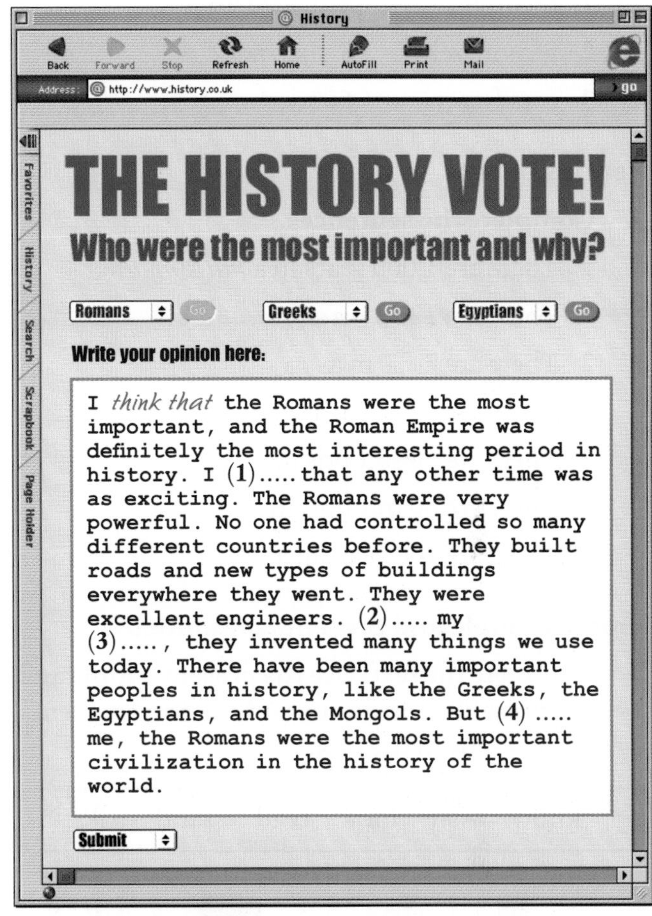

THE HISTORY VOTE!

Who were the most important and why?

Write your opinion here:

I *think that* the Romans were the most important, and the Roman Empire was definitely the most interesting period in history. I (1)..... that any other time was as exciting. The Romans were very powerful. No one had controlled so many different countries before. They built roads and new types of buildings everywhere they went. They were excellent engineers. (2)..... my (3)....., they invented many things we use today. There have been many important peoples in history, like the Greeks, the Egyptians, and the Mongols. But (4)..... me, the Romans were the most important civilization in the history of the world.

6 Think about an interesting period in history. Make notes about these questions:

- When was it?
- What happened?
- Why was it interesting?
- Who were the important people?
- What did they do?

7 Write about the period in history. Use your notes from exercise 6 and expressions from exercise 4.

Finished?

Make a list of important times, people and events in the history of your country.

Progress Check 1

Periods: adjectives

1 Put the letters in the correct order.

inetanc – ancient

1 tacorvini	4 valiedem
2 gea-onrzeb	5 nermdo
3 torsihcperi	6 tneth-yentruc

Periods of time

2 Complete the sentences.

There are 1,000 years in a *millennium*.

1 There are 12 ...... in a year.
2 There are 7 ...... in a ....
3 There are 52 ...... in a ....
4 There are 60 seconds in a ....
5 There are 60 minutes in an ....
6 There are 100 years in a ....

Present simple and present continuous

3 Complete the text. Use the present simple and the present continuous and the correct form of the verbs in the box.

know ~~visit~~ look read stand ask

Maria *visits* the museum every few months. At the moment she (**1**) ..... in front of her favourite object. She (**2**) ..... at it every time she comes here. At the moment she (**3**) ..... a sign about its age and she (**4**) ..... the guide about it. She first saw it two years ago, so she (**5**) ..... that it was 150 million years old then. So why isn't it 150 million and two years old now?

Past simple and past continuous

4 Complete the story. Use the past simple and the past continuous.

Babushka – a Russian myth

One day, three wise men met Babushka while they (**1**) …… (travel). Babushka was a friendly old woman, and she (**2**) …… (give) them food and water, but she (**3**) …… (not want) any money.

Then they told her about their travels. They (**4**) …… (follow) a star. They (**5**) …… (look for) a new king. He was a child. Babushka said, 'I used to have a child, but he (**6**) …… (die).'

After the wise men had left, Babushka (**7**) …… (decide) to follow the star too. She (**8**) … … (want) to take a present for him. She (**9**) …… (not find) the young king, but now she leaves her presents for every child.

Past simple and past perfect

5 Write the sentences. Use the past simple and the past perfect.

1 I / go / to Jenny's birthday party / because she / invite / me.
2 I / not know / her friends because I / not met / them before.
3 Most people / go / home before I / leave.
4 Jenny / phone / me the next day because her friend Alison / ask / about me.
5 Then Alison / call / me because Jenny / give / my phone number to her!

used to

6 Write sentences. Use *used to* and *didn't use to*.

1 She used to be shy.

1 be shy
2 like cameras
3 have long hair
4 wear glasses
5 read a lot
6 be a model

Sally at 10

Sally today

Love life

Have a look!

Find the pages where you:

- **write a letter.**
- **read about love potions.**
- **listen to some friends talking about relationships.**

Vocabulary

Romantic gifts

1 **Listen and repeat. Then translate the names of the gifts.**

VOCABULARY PAGE 125, 2.1

Speaking

2 **Is the chart correct? Do a survey.**

A: When's your birthday?
B: 10th May.
A: Do you like poetry?

ROMANTIC GIFTS

What is the perfect gift for your special friend? Look at his or her star sign to find out.

Aries: 21 Mar–19 Apr
a ticket for the cinema

Libra: 23 Sept–23 Oct
a silver chain

Taurus: 20 Apr–20 May
a poetry book

Scorpio: 24 Oct–21 Nov
a bunch of flowers

Gemini: 21 May–21 Jun
a cuddly toy

Sagittarius: 22 Nov–21 Dec
a box of chocolates

Cancer: 22 Jun–22 Jul
a ring

Capricorn: 22 Dec–19 Jan
a romantic card

Leo: 23 Jul–22 Aug
aftershave or perfume

Aquarius: 20 Jan–18 Feb
a love letter

Virgo: 23 Aug–22 Sept
a romantic novel

Pisces: 19 Feb–20 Mar
a CD of love songs

2a Attraction

Reading

1 Complete texts 1–4 with sentences a–d. Then listen and check.

a This is probably because there are stricter traditions.

b Venus' son, Cupid, has also become a famous symbol for lovers.

c the soldier's lips are now pink.

d They're now in danger of extinction.

2 Read the texts again and answer the questions.

1 What is the connection between animals and love potions?

2 How old was Shadia when she got married?

3 Who married 28 times?

4 Why are Guidarello's lips pink?

5 What does wood symbolize?

6 Why did roses become popular?

Love and ...

1 *Potions*

Love potions probably don't work, but people have made them for thousands of years. Unfortunately, they don't always think about the consequences. The ingredients of love potions often include parts of exotic animals. Sadly, some animals, for example, tigers and rhinos, are still hunted for these ingredients. Hunting has become a serious problem for these animals. ....

2 *Marriage*

Shadia is eighteen years old, but she has already been married for four years. In some parts of the world, it is traditional for people to get married when they are very young. Arranged marriages, where parents choose partners for their children, are also common in some cultures.

In other cultures, people choose their own partners. In fact some people choose again and again and again. One American, Glynn Wolfe, married 28 times, and his last wife, Linda Essex-Wolfe married 23 times. Of course, they are very unusual. Curiously, divorce is less frequent in countries where there are arranged marriages. ....

3 *Kisses*

Are you more interested in love or in money? In the academy of fine arts in Ravenna, Italy, there is a statue of a brave Italian soldier called Guidarello Guidarelli. A superstition says that a woman who kisses the statue will marry a rich man. Tullio Lombardo made the statue in 1525, and over the years, many women have kissed it. People from Ravenna estimate that the statue has had over four million kisses. As a consequence, ...

4 *Symbols*

This couple got married 50 years ago. They've had a long, happy life together. Now they are celebrating their golden wedding anniversary. Each anniversary is symbolized by a different material. They start with paper for the first, and include wood (five years), silver (25 years) and gold (50 years).

Flowers, particularly roses, are also popular gifts for anniversaries, as they have been symbols of love for centuries. The Romans gave each other roses because they believed that they were the favourite flower of Venus, the Roman goddess of love. ....

Exploring grammar

Present perfect and past simple

3 Write a or b for the sentences. Then complete the rules.

a a completed action in the past
b an unfinished period of time

(1) ..... Tullio Lombardo made the statue in 1525.
(2) ..... Over the years, many women have kissed it.
(3) ..... This couple got married sixty years ago.
(4) ..... They've had a long, happy life together.

Rules

We use the present perfect with (1) ..... .
We use the past simple with (2) ..... .

GRAMMAR ▶ PAGES 116–117
IRREGULAR VERBS ▶ INSIDE FRONT COVER

4 Complete the sentences. Use the present perfect or the past simple and the verbs in the box.

be ~~know~~ win enjoy meet
buy not have

I love my wife. We*'ve known* each other a long time, and I (**1**) ...... every moment.

My husband loves his motorbike. He (**2**) ...... it ten years ago and he (**3**) ...... any accidents. He's very careful with it.

My little brother loves Manchester United. Last year, he (**4**) ...... a competition and he (**5**) ...... the team. He (**6**) ...... a big fan since he was four years old.

5 Write about your favourite things. Use the present perfect and the past simple and the ideas in the box.

possession: have (how long?) buy (who?)
friend: know (how long?) meet (where?)
film: watch (how many times?) first see (when?)

My favourite possession is my computer. I've had it since Christmas. My parents bought it for me.

Pronunciation

Weak forms

6 Listen to the weak forms. Then repeat the sentences.

1 /həz/
My brother has got married.

2 /ə/ /əv/
Flowers are symbols of love.

3 /həv bɪn/ /fə/
Roses have been popular for centuries.

7 Listen and write the sentences.

Speaking

8 Work in pairs. Ask and answer questions about the ideas in exercise 5.

possession: Who / buy? How long / had?
friend: How long / know? Where / meet?
film: How many times / watch? When / see it first?

A: What's your favourite possession?
B: My computer.
A: Who bought it for you?

Finished?

Write about other possessions that you like.
My favourite CD is Hot Rap. I've had it since my birthday. My friend gave it to me.

2b Couples

Vocabulary

Relationships

1 Match pictures 1–8 with expressions a–h. Then listen and check.

1 c

a to fall in love with someone
b to get married to someone
c to meet someone
d to go out with someone
e to split up with someone
f to get engaged to someone
g to ask someone out
h to have an argument with someone

VOCABULARY PAGE 125, 2.3

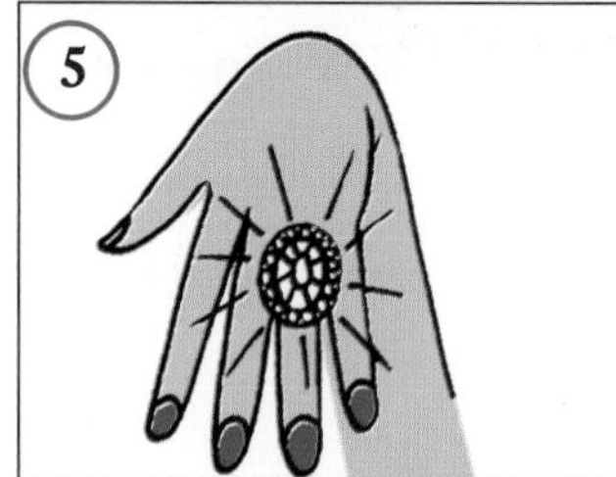

Listening

2 Listen and choose the correct answer.

1 Mary is talking to *Andy / Alex*.
2 Andy was going out with *Mary / Kerry*.
3 *Andy / Alex* has got a new girlfriend.
4 Alex goes out with *Mary / Sue*.

3 Listen and complete the sentences.

1 Mary is looking for Alex because she ...
2 Andy and Kerry ...
3 At the party, Andy ...
4 Kerry was sad but now ...
5 Andy changed a lot after he ...
6 Alex doesn't know who ...

4 Guess what happens next. Choose from sentences a–d. Then listen and check your answers.

I think that ...

a Kerry will ask Alex out.
b Alex will ask Kerry out.
c Kerry will give Alex some bad news.
d Alex will give Kerry some bad news.

Exploring grammar

Present perfect continuous

5 Look at the examples. Then complete the rules with a, b and c.

a *-ing* form **b** present simple **c** past participle

We**'ve been talking** about Andy.
I**'ve been phoning** her all morning.
She **hasn't been answering** her phone.

Rules

We can use the present perfect continuous to talk about an action or repeated actions that started in the past and continued to the present.
We use it to emphasize the activity and the duration of the action.
We form the present perfect continuous with the (1) ...... of the verb **have** + the (2) ...... of the verb **be** + the (3) ...... of the main verb.

GRAMMAR PAGE 117

6 Complete the TV magazine summary. Use the present perfect continuous.

So far this week on

Albert Street

Mary (**1**) ...... (talk) to Alex. She (**2**) ...... (tell) him about Andy at the party. Kerry isn't sad about what has happened because she and Andy (**3**) ...... (not have) a good time. They (**4**) ...... (have) an argument about his friends for a long time. Alex (**5**) ...... (try) to call Sue, but she (**6**) ...... (not answer) the phone. Alex discovers that Andy (**7**) ...... (see) Sue since Saturday and Alex isn't happy ...

Look!

for They have been friends **for** a long time.
since Andy hasn't seen Sue **since** Saturday.

7 Complete the dialogue. Use the present perfect continuous.

Gina: Hi! I haven't seen you for months. *Have you been staying in?*

Yvette: Yeah. A lot!

Gina: Why? What (**1**) ..... you ..... (do)? (**2**) ..... you ..... (study) for the exams in the summer?

Yvette: Yeah, a bit. But money is the main reason.

Gina: Why (**3**) ..... you ..... (save) money?

Yvette: Well, I've got a penfriend, and ...

Gina: Yeah, you showed me his photo. He's really good-looking!

Yvette: He's got a fantastic personality too, and a lovely voice.

Gina: So (**4**) ..... he ..... (phone) you?

Yvette: Yeah, and guess what? I'm going to visit his family in the summer holiday.

Gina: Wow! How long (**5**) ..... he ..... (write) to you now? About a year?

Yvette: One year, two months and ... four days.

Gina: Hmm, I think this is love!

Speaking

8 What have you been doing recently? Ask and answer questions with a partner. Use the ideas in the box plus your own ideas.

go out go to the cinema listen to music
see a new boyfriend / girlfriend
stay in a lot watch TV do homework

What have you been doing recently? Have you been going out?
Yes, I ...

Finished?

What have you and your partner been doing recently? Write some of your activities from your conversation in exercise 8.

Anna's been ...

2c From the heart

Reading

1 Read and listen. Then match authors 1–4 with texts a–d. 

1 a pop group **2** a 19th-century poet **3** a student **4** a soldier on a ship

a *You fear, sometimes, I do not love you so much as you wish? My dear girl, I love you ever and ever and without reserve. The more I have known you the more I have loved. You are always new. The last of your kisses was ever the sweetest; the last smile the brightest.*

ever = always

b
A year has passed since I wrote my note.
But I should have known this right from the start.
Only hope can keep me together.
Love can mend your life
But love can break your heart.

(*Chorus*)
I'll send an SOS to the world. (*x2*)
I hope that someone gets my (*x3*)
Message in a bottle. (*x4*)

c
Dear Wife
I am writing this note on this boat
and dropping it into the sea
just to see if it will reach you.
Ta ta sweet, for the present.
Your hubby

ta ta = goodbye
hubby = husband

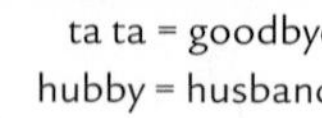

d

TERM PROJECT

Romantic texts

I found three interesting texts. The first was on the internet. I like it because the words are really romantic. It was written by an English poet called John Keats. When he was 23, he met a girl called Fanny, and they fell in love. But Keats knew that he was really sick, so they didn't get married. He died the year after he had written this letter.

The second is from a song that was written over 20 years ago. I heard it on the radio, but I didn't hear all the words. I decided to buy the CD so that I could listen to the song again. I've played it a lot. This verse explains that love can be good or cruel. I agree with that!

The final text was in a newspaper. It's a story with a happier ending than the others, that's why I like it the best. A soldier wrote a message to his wife in 1914. He put the message in a bottle and threw it into the sea. The soldier died, but a fisherman discovered the message in 1999. He found the soldier's daughter and he gave her the letter.

Angela Bennett

2 Put the texts in order of their ages.

1 oldest: ..... **2** ..... **3** ..... **4** most recent: .....

3 Read text d again and answer the questions.

1. Why didn't John Keats get married?
2. How long did the soldier's message stay in the bottle?
3. Which text did Angela find on a website?
4. Which is Angela's favourite text?
5. Why is it her favourite?

Writing

Giving reasons: *so, so that, that's why* and *because*

4 Translate these sentences from Angela's text.

1 I like it **because** the words are really romantic.

2 It's a story with a happier ending than the others, **that's why** I like it the best.

3 I decided to buy the CD **so that** I could listen to the song again.

4 He knew he was really sick, **so** they didn't get married.

5 Choose the correct expressions.

Dear Ben,

This is very hard for me, **so** */* **because** *I'll try to be calm. I'm writing to you (1)* **so / because** *I respect you but I'm afraid that I don't love you, (2)* **so that / so** *we must split up. It's difficult (3)* **so that / because** *we've been together for a long time.*

It's not the end of the world, (4) **so / because** *please don't be sad. I remember when we met and you asked me out (5)* **so that / because** *you liked my smile. I'm sending you this photo (6)* **so that / because** *you won't forget the good times we had together. I'm keeping the ring and the silver chain (7)* **so / because** *they're very special for me.*

Bye, bye Ben. I hope that you'll be happy,

Fran

6 Imagine that you received the letter from Fran. Write a reply. Use *so, so that, that's why,* and *because*.

Explain these things in your letter:

- Do you think that it's a good idea to split up?
  Why?/ Why not?
- Did you enjoy the friendship you had?
  Why?/ Why not?
- How do you feel now?
  Why?
- What are you going to do now?
  Why?

Study skills

Using a dictionary (1): checking pronunciation

The connection between sound and spelling is not regular in English. Dictionaries use symbols so that you can check the pronunciation of new words.

7 Listen and repeat the sounds and words.

/g/	/dʒ/
get married	Gemini
Virgo	arrange

8 Copy and complete the table from exercise 7 with the words in the box.

tiger gift gold marriage message Sagittarius engaged

9 Check your answers to exercise 8 in the Vocabulary pages or in a dictionary.

VOCABULARY PAGE 125

Finished?

Translate some lines from a romantic English song or a poem into your language.

Progress Check 2

Romantic gifts

1 Match pictures 1–7 with the words in the box.

~~ring~~ perfume flowers card chain letter chocolates

1 ring

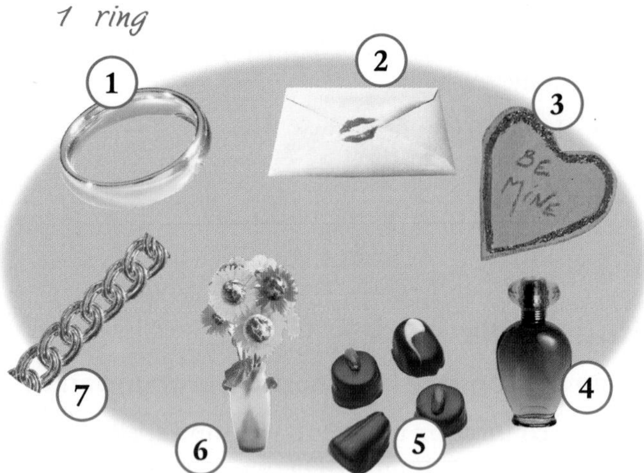

Relationships

2 Put the phrases in chronological order.

1 get engaged, get married

1 get married get engaged
2 go out with someone split up
3 get engaged fall in love
4 have an argument meet someone

Present perfect and past simple

3 Choose the correct form of the verbs.

Dear Jane,
I never felt / **I've never felt** (circled) like this before. (1) **I was** / **I've been** in love with you since the first day that (2) **we met** / **we've met**. (3) **It was** / **It has been** two months ago, on 14th February, a special day! But recently (4) **you were** / **you've been** so cruel! (5) **I wrote** / **I've written** to you every day for the last two weeks, and yesterday (6) **I phoned you** / **I've phoned you** ten times. Why didn't you call me? Tell me, please.
Love, as always,
Carrick

Present perfect continuous

4 Complete the letter. Use the present perfect continuous form of the verbs in the box.

not see ~~live~~ phone go out try look for watch

My family came to Britain from India. We*'ve been living* here for nine years. My dad believes in arranged marriages and my older sister got married two years ago. My dad (**1**) ….. a partner for me, but I've already got a boyfriend. I (**2**) ….. with him for six months. We're in love. I (**3**) ….. him much recently because it's difficult. I (**4**) …... him on my mobile when I can, but my dad (**5**) ….. me. He knows something is wrong. I (**6**) ….. to tell my dad, but it isn't easy. Please help. What should I do?

Priya

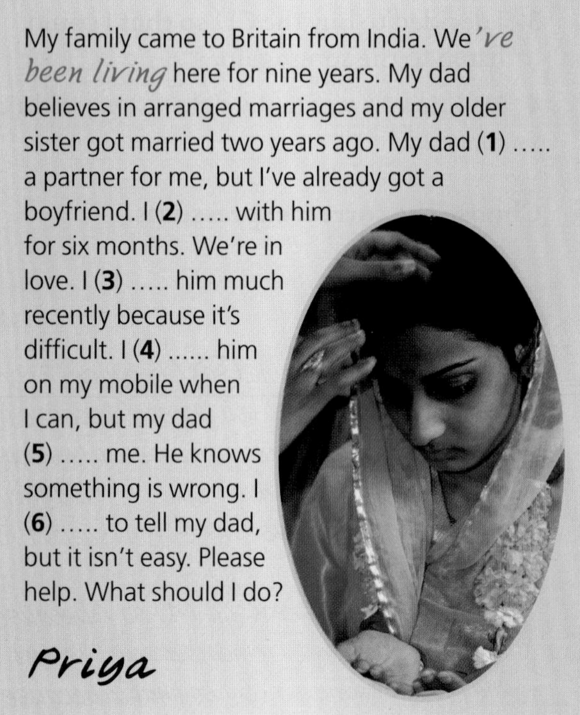

5 Put the words in the correct order.

Priya / been / Has / with a boy? / going out
Has Priya been going out with a boy?
Yes, she has.

1 has / How long / been / seeing / him? / she
For six months.

2 they / been / Where / going?/ have
To the cinema usually.

3 with her dad? / she / been / Has / arguing
No, because her dad doesn't know.

4 her dad / Has / a husband? / trying to find / been
Yes, he has.

5 has / for advice? / asking / Priya / been / Who
She wrote to a magazine and she's talked to her sister.

The World of English 1

Round-up (page 22)

Revision: **Present simple, present continuous, past simple, past continuous, past perfect, *used to*, present perfect, present perfect continuous**

Function: **Inviting people**

1 What does Phil invite Kim to?

Culture File (page 24)

Topic: **Teenagers**

Vocabulary: **Compound nouns**

2 What radio station does Judy listen to?

The Story of Pop (page 26)

Artist: **Queen**

Type of music: **Rock**

Song: **We will rock you**

3 What was the name of Queen's singer?

Round-up 1

Present simple and present continuous

1 Put the verbs in brackets into the present simple or the present continuous.

Adam: Hi Maria, hi John. What are you two doing on the internet?

Maria: We (**1**) .... (look) for web pages for our project on ancient Egypt.

Adam: Egyptian history is fantastic. My father and I really (**2**) .... (enjoy) films and books about Egypt, particularly about Egyptian pharaohs like Tutankhamun and I ....

Maria: Well, today we (**3**) .... (not / study) Egyptian people. I (**4**) .... (write) about the pyramids, and John (**5**) .... (find) some pictures of them on the internet.

John: Well, Adam what (**6**) .... you .... (do) here?

Adam: Me? Oh, I always (**7**) .... (come) here after school. I (**8**) .... (use) the internet every day. It's great.

Past simple, past continuous and *used to*

2 Complete the text with the verbs in the box. Use the past simple, the past continuous and *used to* where possible.

catch	~~live~~	eat	call	fish	talk
stay	wait	go	tell	stop	

My grandparents *used to live* by the sea and when I was a young boy, my brother and I (**1**) .... with them every summer holiday. One day, we were with our granddad on his boat. The boat (**2**) .... quite fast when the engine suddenly (**3**) .... We were in the middle of the sea. Our granddad (**4**) .... for help on his radio. While we (**5**) .... for someone to come our granddad took some fishing lines from a box. He (**6**) .... a lot and had lots of rods and nets. He (**7**).............. us stories when we (**8**) .... a big, beautiful blue and silver fish. It was a very big fish, over 3 kilos, but that night we (**9**) .... it in five minutes!

Past simple and present perfect simple

3 Choose the correct form of the verbs.

I (**1**) *have known / knew* Jim for two years. We (**2**) *haven't met / didn't meet* at a club or at school; we met on the internet! My parents (**3**) *have bought / bought* a new computer with an internet connection two years ago and I wanted to practise my English. I (**4**) *have studied / studied* English since I was little and I enjoy it a lot. I wanted to chat with native speakers and I met Jim at a site about English pop music and we (**5**) *have been / were* friends since then. Jim and his family (**6**) *have visited / visited* me here in Poland twice now, and I (**7**) *'ve been / was* with him and his family in London three times and now we are boy and girlfriend. He (**8**) *has been / was* here last week, but he went home yesterday and now I feel sad!

Present perfect simple and present perfect continuous

4 Put the verbs into the present perfect simple or the present perfect continuous.

Maria, Eva and Tim have invited Philip to dinner. They are getting ready.

Maria: Okay. Tim *has been cooking* (cook) all day and now he's making a cake. We've got drinks. I (**1**).......... (be) to the shops three times and I (**2**) .... (buy) cola and orange juice. What (**3**) .... you .... (do)?

Eva: Me? I (**4**) .... (wash) the dishes for hours!

Maria: You mean you (**5**) .... (not finish)?

Eva: Tim (**6**) .... (use) so many. It's crazy!

Tim: Hey, I've (**7**) .... (work) hard all afternoon.

Eva: And you (**8**) .... (not finish). I know. How much more mess are you going to make?

Maria: Stop arguing you two. I (**9**).......... (have) a text message from Philip. He'll be here in five minutes.

Listening

Inviting someone

1 Put the sentences into the correct order. Then listen and check.

Phil: Oh. Never mind. What exam are you doing? ....

Kim: Hi Phil. No, it's not too bad today. ....

Kim: Sorry, I can't. I've got an exam tomorrow, and I've really got to study. ....

Phil: Hi Kim. It's nice to see you. Is your bag heavy? .*1*.

Phil: Of course. Well, the film's on all week. How about going to see it at the weekend? ....

Phil: Yeah, that sounds good to me! I'll see you on Friday. How about 7 o'clock at the cinema? ....

Kim: OK, great. Then I can celebrate finishing the exam. How about Friday? ....

Phil: Kim, do you fancy going to the cinema tonight? There's a new Brad Pitt film on. ....

Kim: Fine. I'll see you there. ....

Kim: Maths, and I'm very bad at maths. If I don't study, I won't pass it! Brad Pitt will have to wait! ....

Useful expressions

2 Find the expressions in the dialogue. What do they mean?

1 Nice to see you.
2 Do you fancy going to the cinema?
3 How about Friday?
4 That sounds good to me.

3 Make a list of places to go on a date. Use the ideas in pictures 1–4.

1 football match

Dialogue

Asking someone out

4 In pairs, discuss your ideas from exercise 3. Use the dialogue below as a model. Substitute the blue words to form your own dialogues.

D: Listen, Kate, do you fancy going out tonight?
K: No, sorry, Dan. I'm meeting some friends tonight.
D: Well, how about having a coffee sometime?
K: Yes, that sounds good to me. I'll give you my number.
D: OK, great.

Culture File 1

Teenagers 

Vocabulary

Compound nouns: likes and dislikes

1 Read the text. Match definitions 1–5 with words and expressions from the text.

a person who likes staying at home
a home-lover

1 a person who likes going to parties
2 a person who likes music
3 a person who loves animals
4 a person who watches too much television
5 a person who supports Arsenal football club

2 Read the text again. Write five similarities and five differences between you and Judy.

Similarities	Differences
She's 15.	*She likes shopping.*

3 Work in pairs. Ask and answer the questions in the profile.

Profile of a British teenager

Judy Brown is 15 and she lives in Bristol in the west of England.

Judy, are you a home-lover or a party animal?
Well, I go out at weekends. I like shopping and I'm a big cinema-goer. But I'm not mad about parties.

What time do you have to be home?
Normally before eleven o'clock at the weekend, but it depends where I'm going.

Do you help at home?
I wash up sometimes, and I have to tidy my room.

Are you a music fan?
Yes, but I don't like heavy metal. My favourite bands are Gorillaz and Basement Jaxx.

Do you listen to the radio?
I listen to Radio 1 in the morning – it helps me to wake up.

Are you a telly addict?
No, but I watch animal programmes and I like some American series.

So you're an animal-lover?
Yes, definitely.

Have you got a boyfriend?
Not at the moment.

Where did you go for your last holiday?
We stayed in an apartment in Tenerife – there were loads of British people!

Do you get much pocket money?
£40 a month – more if I need clothes. I work on Saturdays in a shoe shop, so I don't usually ask for money.

What do you think of school?
It's OK, but they're too strict about things like jewellery.

What are your ambitions?
I've got GCSEs next year and then I'm going to do A levels. I want to be a vet, so I need good grades for University.

What's your favourite food?
Vegetable lasagne.

Do you like football?
Yes. I'm an Arsenal supporter, like my dad.

What were the last three things you bought?
A magazine, a phone card and some chocolate.

4 **Dan is visiting Britain from the USA. He is talking to Lisa about some of the differences between the two countries. Listen and number the pictures in the order he talks about them.**

Did you know?

- approximately 40% of Americans graduate from college or university.
- 18% of American adults have a passport.
- the average American has 13 days holiday a year.
- 80% of Americans listen to the radio every day.

a holidays

b university

c radio

d pocket money

5 **Listen again. Are the sentences true or false?**

1 Americans watch more TV than British people. ....

2 Americans go on foreign holidays more often than British people. ....

3 Most Americans like to be active on holiday. ....

4 Most American teenagers want to go to university. ....

5 American teenagers usually wear a uniform at school. ....

Project

What are teenagers like in your country? Make a poster about the teen culture in your town. Use the ideas in the box and add other information that you think is important.

- music
- books and magazines
- clubs
- TV and radio programmes
- hobbies and interests
- sports

Include photos and drawings.

The Story of Pop 1

Rock

1 Read and listen. Then answer the questions.

1. What are the characteristics of hard rock and heavy metal?
2. Why did rock 'supergroups' need a lot of equipment?
3. Were Queen more popular than The Beatles in Britain?
4. What type of music did Queen play?
5. Why did Queen fans go to a memorial concert?

Rock

Rock music, especially hard rock and heavy metal, has got a hard guitar sound, a heavy beat and loud vocals. Hard rock became popular in the 1970s, as groups started to play louder and faster.

The 1970s and '80s was the era of the first rock 'supergroups'. Bands started to play in bigger places, usually sports stadiums. As the concerts became bigger, the groups needed more lights, more exciting effects and bigger sound systems.

Queen

Queen started in 1972, playing very small concerts. Ten years later, they were a supergroup, playing in sports stadiums in Europe, Japan, the USA and Latin America. They were one of the most successful groups of the last 30 years. In Britain, they were voted the second most popular band of the millennium, after The Beatles. They played both hard rock and pop. In 1991, their lead singer, Freddie Mercury, died of AIDS. More than 75,000 fans went to his memorial concert.

2 Complete the song. Use the words in the box. Then listen and check.

place (*x 3*)   face (*x 3*)   man (*x 5*)   ~~boy~~

We will rock you

Buddy, you're a *boy* make a big noise
Playing in the street gonna be a big (**1**) ......
some day.

You got mud on your (**2**) ....
You big disgrace.
Kicking your can all over the (**3**) ....
Singing

(Chorus)
We will, we will rock you.
We will, we will rock you.

Buddy, you're a young (**4**) ......
hard (**5**) ....
Shouting in the street gonna take on
the world some day.
You got blood on your (**6**) ....
You big disgrace.
Waving your banner all over the (**7**) ....
Singing

(Repeat chorus)

Buddy, you're an old (**8**) ...... poor (**9**) ......
Pleading with your eyes going to make
you some peace some day.
You got mud on your (**10**) ....
You big disgrace.
Somebody better put you
back in your (**11**) ....

(Repeat chorus)

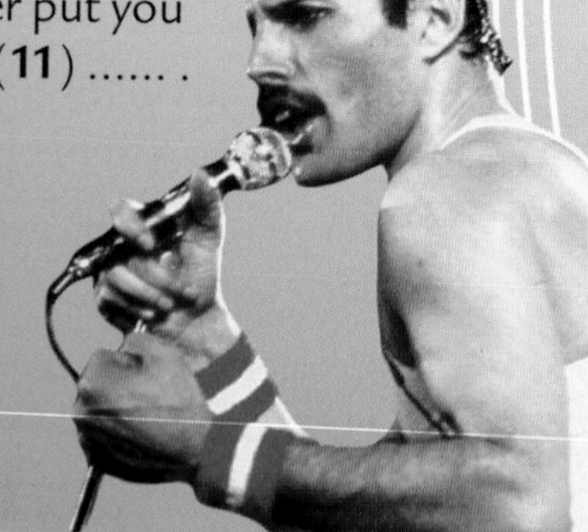

Glossary
buddy (USA) = friend (UK)

Campaign

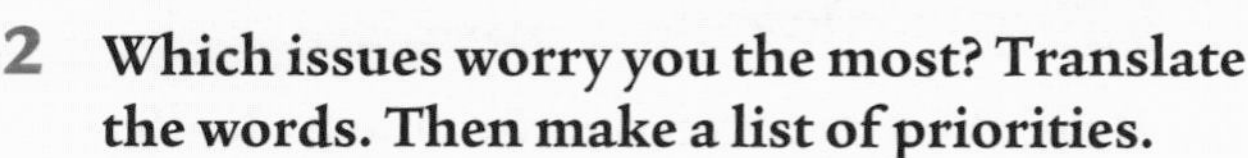

Find the pages where you:
- **read information about different charities.**
- **write a letter to a company.**
- **listen to a debate about genetic engineering.**

Vocabulary
World issues

1 **Match pictures 1–8 with the words in the box. Then listen and repeat.**

disease ~~animal rights~~ famine genetic engineering poverty terrorism the environment war

1 animal rights

2 **Which issues worry you the most? Translate the words. Then make a list of priorities.**

VOCABULARY PAGE 125, 3.1

Speaking

3 **Work in pairs. Make a list of priorities for your country. Use the words in the box.**

more most not very quite very

A: Do you think that animal rights are important in our country?
B: Yes, they're quite important – but disease is a more serious issue.

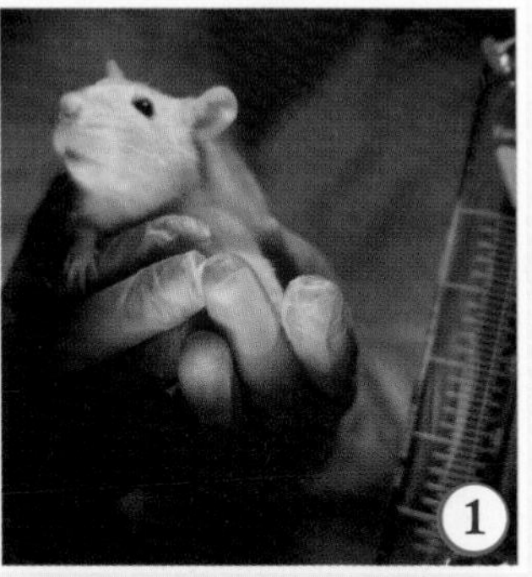

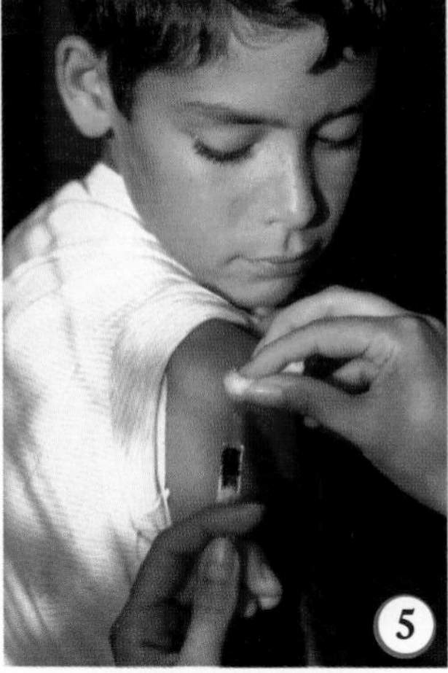

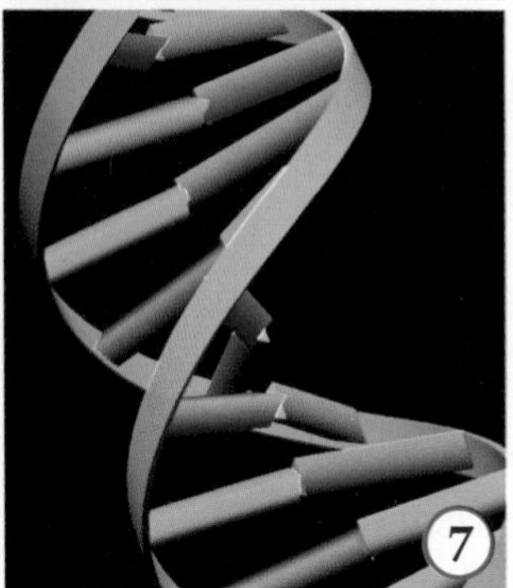

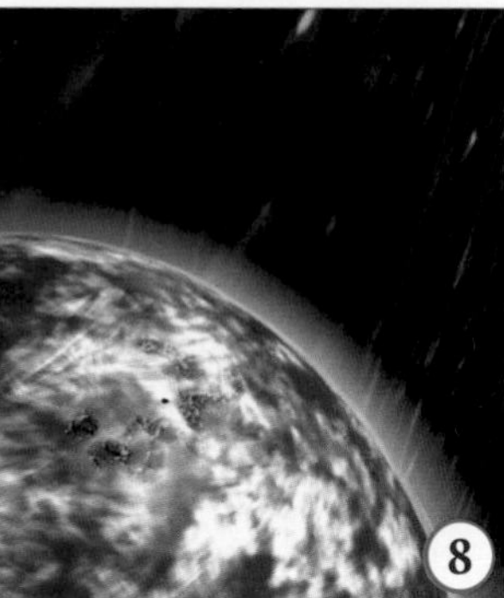

3a Charity

Vocabulary

Causes

1 Listen and repeat. Then translate the words into your language.

collection box charity slogan placard sticker boycott petition leaflet demonstration banner government

VOCABULARY PAGE 125, 3.2

Reading

2 Read the extracts from the charity leaflets. Which of the charities (1–3) is each speaker (a–c) going to help? Listen and check.

1 There are around 14,000 new cases of AIDS every day. The virus will infect millions of people in the next ten years. In some places, the epidemic is out of control, and is an additional burden on top of poverty, famine and poor health. At the moment, nearly 50% of victims are women and children. We believe that this number will increase.

2 I've worked in many parts of the developing world. Our organization and others respond to emergencies resulting from environmental disasters, wars and conflict. It's a huge task, and without more doctors and money many people who desperately need our help won't survive.

3
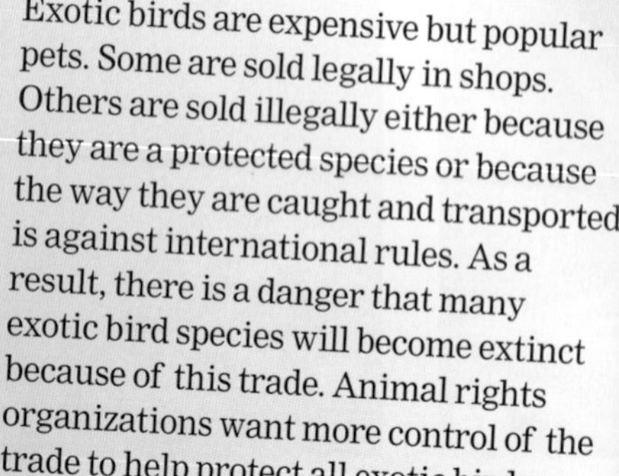
Exotic birds are expensive but popular pets. Some are sold legally in shops. Others are sold illegally either because they are a protected species or because the way they are caught and transported is against international rules. As a result, there is a danger that many exotic bird species will become extinct because of this trade. Animal rights organizations want more control of the trade to help protect all exotic birds.

3 Read the texts again and answer the questions.

1 Why does Elaine think that AIDS victims have more problems?
2 How many new cases of AIDS are there every day?
3 What problems have charity organizations got in the developing world?
4 Why is Barry angry with the government?
5 Why are exotic birds sold?
6 What is Fiona going to do about the problem of illegal exotic pets?

a Fiona, 16

I like animals and in our family we've got two tropical birds. I didn't know that it was illegal to sell these birds. I'm going to tell my friends and I'm going to protest outside pet shops where they sell birds illegally. I've already made a placard. I'm going to explain the problem and ask people to sign a petition. I'm sure people will help.

b Elaine, 17

I think that a lot of people don't really understand the disease, so those with the disease have a lot more problems. People are scared of them, but they shouldn't be worried. At our school, we've had a really good idea. We've got a collection box from an AIDS charity, and we're having a special collection all next week. The collection starts on Monday morning. We're going to ask people in the street too.

c Barry, 20

I'm angry. We see the same sad images on TV all the time. It's the government's responsibility to help people in emergency situations. The Prime Minister is coming to our town on Monday, so we're having a demonstration outside the university. The university opens at 9.00. The demonstration begins at 8.30, so everyone will see it when they arrive. Then we're going to give a letter to the Prime Minister.

Exploring grammar

Talking about the future: *will, going to,* present continuous and present simple

4 Look at the example sentences. Then complete the rules with *will, going to,* the present continuous and present simple.

The virus **will** infect millions of people.
I'm going to protest outside pet shops.
The Prime Minister **is coming** to our town.
The university **opens** at 9.00.

Rules

We use (1) ...... for plans and intentions.
We use (2) ...... for predictions.
We use the (3) ...... for arrangements.
We use the (4) ...... for timetables and schedules.

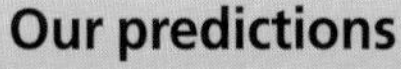
GRAMMAR PAGE 117

5 Choose the correct verb forms.

Please help EARTH CAMPAIGN

The world's climate

Our predictions

The climate of the world is changing because of air pollution. Scientists predict that temperatures are **going to increase / will increase** in the next decade and this **(1) is going to cause / will cause** very serious problems. One possibility is that more of the Earth **(2) is going to become / will become** desert.

Dear Jake

I'm sending you this leaflet so that you can show it to your teachers. Our school is going to help Earth Campaign, and we've planned a project for next term.

(3) We're going to try / We'll try to save energy because energy production causes a lot of air pollution. Recycling saves energy, so **(4) we're going to recycle / we'll recycle** paper and cans. **(5) We're going to make / We'll make** stickers and posters to publicize the problem.

Can your school help too?

Love, Tessa

6 Complete the dialogue. Use the present simple and the present continuous.

Jake: I'*m having* a party on Saturday. Do you want to come?

Tessa: Sorry, I can't. I (**1**) ...... (go) to London this weekend.

Jake: OK, how about meeting after school on Friday?

Tessa: No, I won't be here. School (**2**) .... (finish) at four o'clock, then my mum (**3**) ...... (drive) me to the station. My train (**4**) ...... (leave) at five. I (**5**) ...... (stay) with my aunt. She (**6**) ...... (take) me to a demonstration.

Jake: Is it for Earth Campaign?

Tessa: Yeah, that's right. It (**7**) ...... (start) at nine in the morning, so I have to go on Friday evening. It's about recycling and saving energy.

Jake: But your trip to London will use a lot of energy, won't it?

Tessa: Hmm – that's true! I hadn't thought of that!

Pronunciation

-tion

7 Listen, repeat and mark the stress on the words.

1 collection
2 demonstration
3 petition
4 pollution
5 organization
6 situation

Finished?

Design placards and posters for the issues in exercises 2 and 5.

3b Debate

Reading

1 Read the TV guide. Then complete the text with the words in the box.

instructions ~~cells~~ genes disease manipulated clone

On TV Tonight Channel 4 20.45

Debate: Genetic engineering

Tonight's guests on *Debate* are:

Dr Leo Nuttall, a scientist specializing in genetic engineering.

Mark Tanner, an ecologist working for a well-known environmental charity.

Genetic engineering is the focus of a lot of discussion. Tonight's programme examines some of the issues.

Plants and animals are made up of *cells* which contain nuclei made up of a chemical called DNA. Genes are pieces of DNA which control what the organism looks like and how it functions. In other words, genes give organisms **(1)** ...... – about eye colour, whether it has wings or arms, needles or leaves and thousands of other characteristics.

Normally, an organism inherits its characteristics through its genes. However, scientists have discovered that the genetic make-up of an organism can be **(2)** ...... to change the genetic information that they contain. In plants this means we can create bigger strawberries, greener apples, and cereals which are resistant to **(3)** .... We can even make tomatoes frost resistant by inserting genes from fish. It is also possible to duplicate an organism, creating a **(4)** .... Dolly the sheep was famous because she was the first clone of a farm animal.

But what will happen if we continue this manipulation in plants and animals? How do plants cope with animal genes and vice versa? And what will happen if we modify human **(5)** ......? What will happen if cloning is not controlled by strict rules? Is this an extension of traditional breeding methods or something much darker? Listen to the experts in tonight's debate about genetic engineering.

Listening

2 Read opinions 1–5 and guess who says them. Write *Dr Nuttall* or *Mark Tanner*.

1 Dr Nuttall

1 If we create better cereals, we'll help solve food problems in the developing world.

2 If we modify some genes in a plant, the plant will become more productive.

3 If we don't experiment, we'll never make progress.

4 If you modify one gene, other genes will change as a result.

5 If we continue experimenting, we'll create monsters.

3 Listen and check your answers to exercise 2.

4 Put the opinions in the order you hear them.

a Some crops have lower nutritional value when they are genetically modified. ....

b Animals can't choose whether they take part in experiments. ....

c There is a possibility of mutations. ....

d I think genetic engineering is a good thing. ....

e Farmers have been changing the genetic make up of their crops for centuries. ....

f We're just trying to help nature. ....

Exploring grammar

First conditional

5 Look at the example and complete the table with *will* / *won't*, the infinitive and present simple.

If a cereal **is** more productive, we'**ll have** more food.

Action	Consequence
If + (1) ...... ,	(2) ...... + (3) ......

GRAMMAR PAGE 118

6 Complete the sentences. Use the first conditional.

If scientists *clone* animals, we*'ll have* more food.

1 If we ...... (clone) humans, people ...... (be) identical.
2 If we ...... (not protest), people ...... (not know) about the problems.
3 If people ...... (not understand), then nothing ...... (change).
4 If we ...... (experiment) with nature, we ...... (pay) the consequences.
5 If scientists ...... (stop) working, our lives ...... (not improve).
6 If we ...... (not help) the developing world, people ...... (die).

7 Complete the sentences with your ideas.

If the government bans tobacco in the future, *people will live longer.*

1 I'll be happy in the future if ....
2 I won't be happy in the future if ....
3 If I live for 100 years, ...
4 We'll destroy the environment if ....
5 If we don't stop wars, ...
6 If scientists create human clones, ...

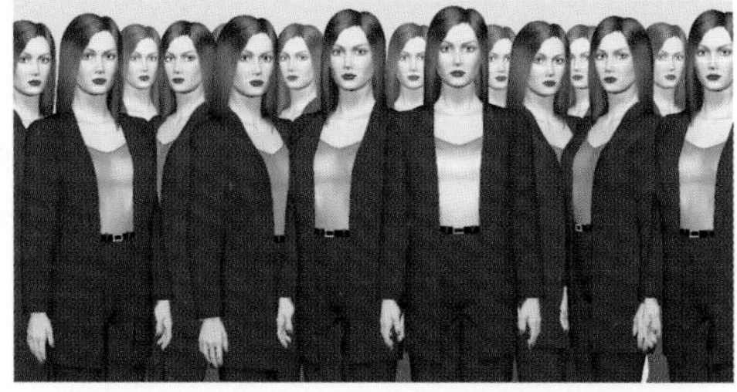

Future time clauses: *before*, *when* and *after*

8 Look at the examples and complete the rule.

Before we start the debate, can you explain a little about genetic engineering?
When we have better cereals, we can solve the world's food problems.
Are you going to clone humans **after you have cloned** more animals?

Rule

We use the **present** / **future** tense with **before** and **when** to talk about the future. We often use the present perfect with **after**.

GRAMMAR PAGE 118

9 Complete the politicians' promises. Use the correct form of the verbs in the box.

win ~~be~~ stop clone be have

When I*'m* Prime Minister, I'll stop genetic engineering. We should stop genetic engineering before scientists (**1**) ...... humans.

After I (**2**) ...... the next election, I'll give more money to scientists. They'll solve all our problems when they (**3**) ...... more money.

We must save the environment before it (**4**) ..... too late! When we (**5**) .... global warming, the world will be a safer place.

Finished?

Imagine that you are a politician. What will you do if you win the next election?

3c A good cause

Reading

1 Look at the picture and answer the questions.

1 Where is the boy?

2 What is he doing?

2 Read and listen to Cindy's diary. Check your answers to exercise 1.

24 April

Last night I saw a documentary about the tough lives of street children in India. The TV cameras followed a gang of young people. Some of the children were abandoned and didn't know where their parents were. Others were orphans. They were living in a shanty town close to a rubbish dump. Every day they looked in the rubbish for food and for stuff that they could sell or use. They were dependent on drugs. Some of them were very sick or dying.

The programme showed the same group of children three months later. Volunteers from a charity organization were now working with them, and the children were living in rooms in a hostel. They were still working at the dump, but they were selling materials to a recycling company. They were saving the money they were making and not spending it on drugs. Their lives were still difficult, but thanks to the charity, they had a chance.

The presenter of the programme explained the work of the charity and made an appeal to the audience. It was very emotional. He said that a lot of street kids are in danger of dying because of people's apathy. He's right. If we don't do anything, then this situation won't change. I'm going to do something to help.

3 Read the text again and answer the questions.

1 Where do the children live?

2 How do the street children find food?

3 Where were they living three months later?

4 What were they doing with their money?

5 What did the presenter say in his appeal?

6 What did Cindy decide?

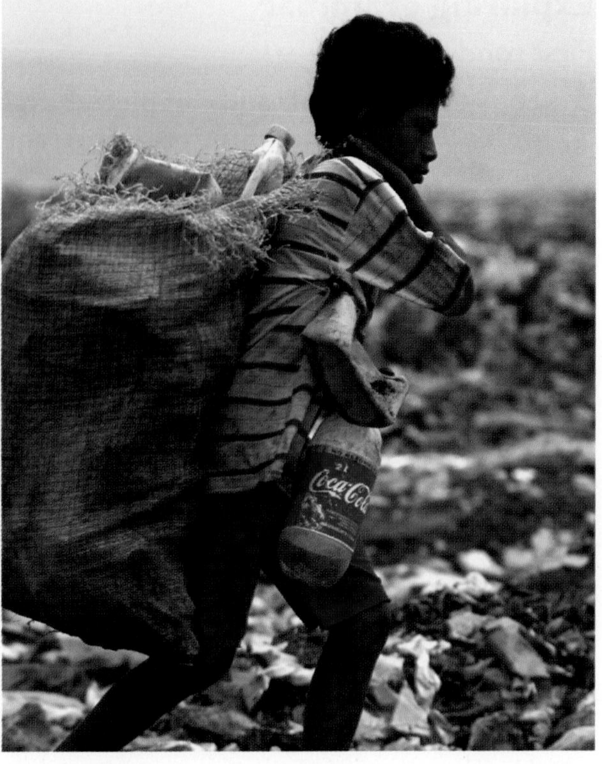

Study skills

Using a dictionary (2): finding the best definition

4 Read the instructions.

Look at the word *close* in context:

- What part of speech is the word? Is it a noun, verb, adjective, adverb or preposition?

They were living in a shanty town close to the rubbish dump.

Look up the dictionary definition of *close*. Choose the most appropriate definition.

Look at the word *close* again in context. Is your definition logical?

5 Find these words in the text in exercise 2. Then use a dictionary to find the best definition.

1 abandoned	(line 4)	5 company	(line 15)
2 orphans	(line 5)	6 chance	(line 17)
3 stuff	(line 7)	7 appeal	(line 19)
4 materials	(line 14)	8 right	(line 21)

Listening

6 Listen to Cindy and Damian's phone conversation. Complete the sentences with *Pete, Damian, Cindy* or *Tania*.

1 ...... has organized a disco.

2 ...... is going to work as a security guard at the disco.

3 ...... is going to make T-shirts and sell them.

4 ...... is going to do a cycle marathon.

7 Listen again and answer the questions.

1 Has the school agreed to the disco yet?

2 How much is the DJ going to cost?

3 What is written on the T-shirts?

4 Who chose the route for the cycle marathon?

5 Are people definitely going to give Cindy the money?

6 Is Cindy confident that she can finish the cycle marathon?

Writing

Planning your writing

Your writing will be clearer and more effective if you plan it.

8 Look at Cindy's writing plan. Read her letter and put parts a–g in the correct order.

Introduction (paragraph 1)
- reason for writing

Situation (paragraph 2)
- present situation
- consequence of positive action
- consequence of no action

Plan of action (paragraph 3)
- what I'm going to do to help
- what others can do to help

Concluding remarks (paragraph 4)
- thanks to the reader

a I'm going to do a cycle marathon in June in aid of a charity which helps these people. I'm looking for sponsors. If you can donate any money, please contact me at the above address.

b Lewins Department Store
1 High Street
Oxford
OX1 3CP

Dear Sir or Madam,

c 63 Whitedale Road
Oxford
OX4 9DY
29th May

d Yours faithfully,
Cindy Black

e I am collecting money for a good cause, and I am writing to ask for your support.

f There are many young people in India who live on the street. They try to sell things that they find in rubbish dumps, and their lives are very difficult. If we help these young people, they will have a better chance in life. If we don't help them, a lot of them will turn to drugs.

g I hope to hear from you. Thank you for taking the time to read my letter.

9 Think of a good cause and activities to raise money. Write a letter of appeal. Use Cindy's plan.

Finished?

Think of different ways to make money for a good cause.

1 Do a sponsored swim.

Progress Check 3

World issues

1 Complete the sentences with the words in the box.

poverty ~~terrorism~~ disease
animal rights the environment war
famine genetic engineering

Terrorism causes many deaths.

1 Vegetarians think that ...... are important.
2 Malaria is a serious ....
3 ...... is the opposite of peace.
4 ...... hurts the poorest people in all countries.
5 ...... happens when there isn't enough food.
6 ...... tries to produce new types of plants.
7 Global warming is damaging ....

Causes

2 Complete the words with the missing vowels.

1 b _ nn _ r 3 l _ _ fl _ t 5 st _ ck _ r
2 ch _ r _ ty 4 sl _ g _ n 6 pl _ c _ rd

will and *going to*

3 Choose the correct forms of the verbs.

Interview with Thor, guitarist with The Bones.

TVM: Thor, what are your plans for the summer?

Thor: Well, **I'm going to / I'll have a** good time, as always! (1) **I'll / I'm going to** have a holiday. I've already bought the tickets.

TVM: Have you got any plans for concerts this year?

Thor: Well, The Bones (2) **will / are going to** play one concert this year. It's a charity special. We've decided (3) **we'll / we're going to** give a lot of the money we make to animal charities.

TVM: How do you think that the concert will go?

Thor: I think that if the weather's good, (4) **we'll / we're going to** have a great time. The organizers predict that about 100,000 people (5) **will / are going to** watch it.

Present simple and present continuous

4 Look at Anna's information and write sentences. Use the present simple and the present continuous.

Bus timetable

(1) Leave: Bow Street	Arrive: town centre
6.30	7.00

(2) meet Jim at the Rock Club Bones concert –
(3) start 7.30,
(4) finish 10.00
(5) take Jim to the vegetarian café

1 The bus *leaves at 6.30.*
2 Anna ...
3 The concert ...
4 The concert ...
5 Anna ...

First conditional

5 Complete the sentences. Use the first conditional forms of the verbs.

If Anna *misses* the bus, she*'ll be* late.

1 If she ...... (not be) on time, Jim ...... (have to) wait.
2 If The Bones ...... (be) popular, the concert ...... (be) full.
3 If people ...... (not go), The Bones ...... (not make) any money.
4 If The Bones ...... (make) a lot money, they ...... (give) it to charity.
5 If Anna ...... (like) The Bones' concert, she ...... (buy) their CD.

Future time clauses: *before, after* and *when*

6 Write sentences about Anna's evening.

Before Anna / catch / the bus, she'll finish her homework.
Before Anna catches the bus, she'll finish her homework.

1 After Anna / meet / Jim, they're going to a concert.
2 Before they / see / The Bones, they'll have to buy tickets.
3 When they / leave / the concert, they're going to a café.

Looks

Have a look!

Find the pages where you:

- **present the results of a questionnaire.**
- **read about the work of an image consultant.**
- **listen to two people describe a clothes nightmare.**

Vocabulary

Body art

1 **Match pictures 1–8 with the words in the box. Then listen and repeat.**

wig contact lenses hairstyle
jewellery cosmetic surgery piercing
tattoo make-up

VOCABULARY PAGE 126, 4.1

Speaking

2 **In pairs, ask and answer questions about the people in the pictures. Use the words in the box to help you.**

horrible stylish cool boring creative
interesting attractive out of the ordinary

A: What do you think of her hairstyle?
B: I think it's horrible.

1 2 3 4 5 6 7 8

4a A new look

Reading

1 **Listen and read. Why do Gary and Meg want to change their image?**

2 **Read the text again and answer the questions.**

1 How does Louise decide what advice to give to clients?
2 How do image consultants use computers?
3 What type of person uses an image consultant?
4 What is Louise's opinion about Gary's earrings?
5 What is Louise's opinion about Meg's weight?

Changing **faces**

Do you want to change your image? If the answer is 'yes', why not go to an image consultant? In Britain, there are now more than 2,000 consultants advising people about their image. But don't forget to take your credit card. Top image consultants can cost £200 an hour!

Reporter Bella Wigan went to investigate their work.

Bella: What service do you offer your clients?

Louise: Well, we advise clients on their image. We analyse the shape of the client's face and body so that we can tell them which clothes and hairstyle will suit them best. We also look at their skin and hair colour, and we tell them which colours are the best for them to wear.

Bella: Do you use computers?

Louise: Yes, with computer images we can show a client how they would look if they changed their image.

Bella: Who are your clients?

Louise: Our clients vary a lot. We've had a lot of different people: politicians and business executives, and anyone who simply wants a change, to get a better job, or to find a partner!

Bella: I've got some photos of friends here. Could you give me your opinion? Both of them want to improve their image.

Louise: Yes, of course. I need to know a little bit about them first. Why do they want to change their image?

Bella: Well, Gary is trying to get a job in TV.

Louise: Well, if he had shorter hair, he'd look smarter. Also if he didn't wear earrings, he would be suitable for more jobs. At the moment he doesn't look serious enough for some programmes.

Bella: What about Meg? She's bored with her image and wants a more interesting look.

Louise: Well, if she wore brighter colours, she'd feel better. In the photo, she's wearing very ordinary casual clothes. She'd look more interesting in something a bit more individual.

Bella: What about her hair?

Louise: She needs a really good hair cut. She has nice eyes. If she had shorter hair you would notice them more.

Bella: What do you think about her weight?

Louise: I think that if she put some weight on, she'd be prettier. She's a bit too thin.

Bella: Well thank you for that. I'm sure Meg and Gary will be interested to hear your comments.

Exploring grammar

Second conditional

We use the second conditional to express a hypothesis (the consequence of a possible action).

3 Look at the table. Then complete the rule with *past simple* and *infinitive*.

Action	Consequence
If he **had** shorter hair,	he**'d look** smarter.
If she **wore** brighter clothes,	she**'d feel** better.
If she **lost** more weight,	she **wouldn't** be as pretty.
Rule	
Action	**Consequence**
If + (1) ...... , +	would + (2) ......

GRAMMAR ▶ PAGE 118

4 Complete the sentences. Use the second conditional.

If I *had* more money, I*'d buy* some new clothes.

1 If I ...... (have) new clothes, I ...... (go out).
2 If I ...... (go out) more, I ...... (meet) more people.
3 If I ...... (meet) more people, I ...... (be) happier.
4 If I ...... (be) happier, I ...... (feel) more confident.
5 If I ...... (feel) more confident, I ...... (look for) a better job.
6 If I ...... (find) a better job, I ...... (have) more money.

5 Complete the sentences with your ideas.

If I wanted to look different, I*'d change the colour of my hair.*

1 I'd buy expensive clothes if ...
2 If I had cosmetic surgery, my parents ...
3 I'd wear crazy clothes if ...
4 I wouldn't be surprised if ...
5 My friends wouldn't believe it if ...
6 If I was a pop star, I ...
7 If I could choose any job, I ...
8 My parents would be angry if ...

Speaking

6 Work in pairs. Talk about what you would do if you won the lottery.

If I won the lottery, I'd buy lots of clothes.

Pronunciation

Silent consonants

7 Listen and repeat. Circle the silent consonants.

1 would	4 height	7 calm
2 wouldn't	5 knee	8 castle
3 weight	6 foreign	

8 Listen and repeat. Then write the phrases.

> **Finished?**
> Write your ideas and your partner's ideas from exercise 6.

4b Appearances

Vocabulary

Describing clothes: adjectives

1 Find pairs of opposites.

patterned – plain

~~patterned~~ comfortable tight fashionable scruffy dark unfashionable smart ~~plain~~ uncomfortable bright baggy

Look!

un-

My old jeans are not comfortable.

They are **un**comfortable.

2 Listen and check. Repeat the words.

VOCABULARY PAGE 126, 4.4

Amber Craig

3 Read the information and look at the pictures. Describe the people's clothes.

Listening

4 Listen to Amber and Craig's stories. Where did each person go? Did they feel good or bad in the end?

5 Listen again and answer the questions.

1 Who bought Amber's dress?
2 Why did she wear the dress?
3 When did she know that her clothes were too smart?
4 Where did Craig go after the beach?
5 What had he forgotten?
6 Why didn't he change his clothes?

Speaking

6 Work in pairs. Ask and answer the questions.

1 Is it better for clothes to be comfortable or fashionable?
2 Is it more fashionable to wear tight clothes or baggy clothes?
3 Do you know anyone who wears really colourful clothes? Describe some of their clothes
4 Do you prefer to wear bright or dark colours?
5 When do you have to wear smart clothes?
6 When do you like wearing something scruffy?

Clothes nightmares

6.45pm, C4

Sometimes appearances can be important. So what happens when you really are wearing the wrong clothes?

Amber and Craig tell us about their worst clothes nightmares.

Exploring grammar

Third conditional

We use the third conditional to talk about actions and consequences in the past. The actions and consequences did not happen.

7 Look at the examples then complete the rule with *would / wouldn't*, *past perfect*, *past participle* and *have*.

If the dress **had been** cheap, I **wouldn't have worn** it.
(= But the dress wasn't cheap, so I wore it.)
If I **had had** time, I **would have changed**.
(= But I didn't have time, so I didn't change.)

Rule

A third conditional sentence includes an action and a consequence.

Action	Consequence
If + (1) ……,	(2) …… + (3) …… + (4) ……

GRAMMAR PAGE 118

IRREGULAR VERBS INSIDE FRONT COVER

8 Complete the dialogue.

have had ~~hadn't~~ chosen would realized

Paul: Hi, Tim! You don't usually come here!

Tim: I know, I hate discos, but I'm meeting Liz here. If she *hadn't* asked me, I wouldn't (**1**) …… come. Do you know where she is?

Paul: No, there are too many people here. I can't find her. But she can't miss you in that T-shirt. It's so bright!

Tim: I put it on so she'd see me. But if I had (**2**) …… how many people were coming I (**3**) …… have arranged to meet her outside.

Liz: Hi! Oh no, Tim! Your T-shirt! I would have (**4**) …… something different if I (**5**) …… known!

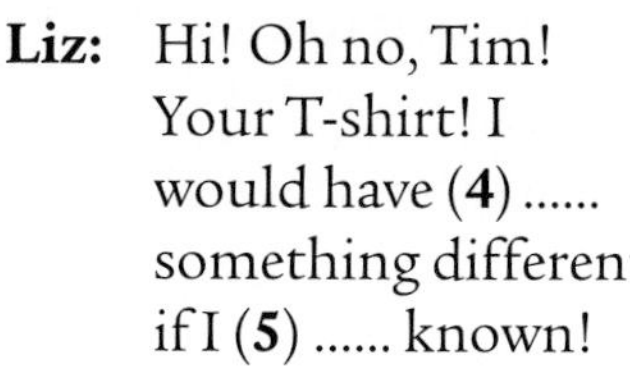

9 Write sentences. Use the third conditional.

If I (be) there, I (see) you.
If I'd been there, I would have seen you.

1. If I (have) more money, I (buy) the boots I saw yesterday.
2. If my trousers (not be) baggy, they (not fall down).
3. I (feel) more comfortable at the interview if my jacket (not be) tight.
4. I (be) fashionable if I (live) in the 1980s.
5. If your boyfriend (not wear) scruffy clothes, we (invite) him.
6. My parents (feel) bad if I (not wear) a smart dress.

too, *so* and *such*

10 Look at the examples and complete the rules with *too*, *so* and *such*.

It was **too** big for me.
I felt **so** uncomfortable.
We had **such** a good evening.

Rules

We use **too**, **so** and **such** for emphasis.
We don't use **too** when we say positive things.
We use (1) …… or (2) …… before an adjective.
We use (3) …… before **a** / **an** + adjective + noun.

GRAMMAR PAGE 118

11 Complete the dialogue with *too*, *so* and *such*.

Jo: That T-shirt is so nice. It's (**1**) …… an interesting colour. And I like your hairstyle – it's (**2**) …… original.

Sam: Really? The T-shirt was (**3**) …… cheap, I couldn't believe it. I was (**4**) …… lucky. But I cut my hair myself because the hairdresser was (**5**) …… expensive.

Finished?

Write about the type of clothes you like to wear.

4c Fashion victims

Reading

1 Look at pictures 1–4. Then read and listen. In what order are the things mentioned in the text?

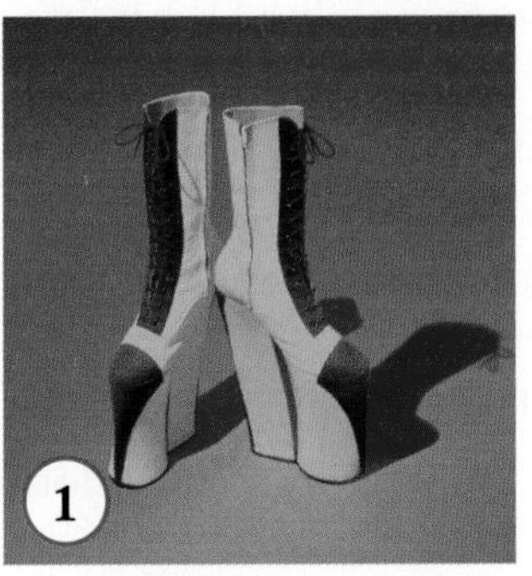
1

2

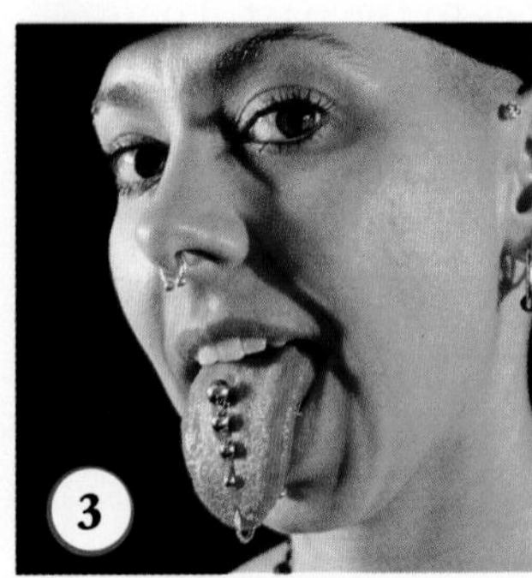
3

4

Fashion victims

Ouch! I feel pain when I see a pierced tongue or a tattoo! Why do people do it? Well, piercing and tattoos have been popular for thousands of years. People have used them as religious or magic symbols, and to identify tribes, prisoners, priests, slaves, gangs and other groups. And people also used them simply to decorate their bodies. The history of fashion is often painful – people have always suffered in order to look better.

You probably think, for example, that uncomfortable platform shoes were a twentieth century invention. Wrong! In the sixteenth century, in southern Europe, people were wearing shoes called 'chopines', which were sometimes 30 centimetres high. Platform shoes were also popular 100 years later in France, probably because King Louis XIV, who wasn't very tall, liked wearing them.

Later, in the seventeenth and eighteenth centuries, rich people thought that washing was unhealthy. They used a lot of perfume to hide the smell of their bodies and they covered their dirty faces with thick make-up and 'beauty spots'. Hair was only washed twice a year, so wigs also became very fashionable. The best wigs were made from human hair, but a cheaper alternative was horse hair. Richer people wore bigger wigs, and sometimes the wigs were incredibly uncomfortable. In the nineteenth century, women suffered more than men. They wore incredibly tight corsets and huge skirts, making it difficult to sit down or to eat.

Today, we're still slaves to fashion. Although clothes are more comfortable, we are now influenced a lot by the media, which is full of men and women with 'perfect' bodies. Unfortunately, a lot of young people think that these models really are perfect. Three and a half million people (male and female) in Britain suffer from eating disorders, like bulimia or anorexia. Cosmetic surgery has also become popular. This type of surgery is sometimes necessary, but today many people have cosmetic surgery simply because they aren't happy with their appearance. Cosmetic surgery can be expensive and it can go wrong and cause health problems. About 70,000 people have cosmetic surgery in Britain every year: a very painful statistic. Ouch!

2 Read the text again and answer the questions.

1 Why have people used piercing and tattoos in the past?

2 Why did King Louis XIV wear platform shoes?

3 Why did wigs become popular in the seventeenth and eighteenth centuries?

4 Does the writer think that today's clothes are uncomfortable?

5 Do men suffer from eating disorders?

6 Does the writer think that the statistics for cosmetic surgery are acceptable?

Speaking

3 **Work in pairs. Ask and answer the questions. Then tell your teacher the results. Find the total result for the class.**

Fashion victims questionnaire

1. Would you buy a magazine because of the beautiful people on the cover?
   a Yes b No
2. Would you get a tattoo if all of your friends had one?
   a Yes b No
3. Would you wear uncomfortable shoes if they were trendy?
   a Yes b No
4. Would you go out with someone if they were badly dressed?
   a Yes b No
5. Would you always buy designer-label clothes if you had the money?
   a Yes b No
6. Would you be embarrassed if your mum or dad had a pierced tongue?
   a Yes b No

Writing

A report: presenting statistics

4 **Look at the graph and complete the report. Use the words in the box. Then listen and check.**

Most people | Everybody | One or two people | About half | ~~Nobody~~ | A few people

Fashion victims report

We interviewed 20 people in our fashion victims questionnaire.

- (**1**) *Nobody* said that they would buy a magazine because of the beautiful people on the cover.
- (**2**) …… said that they would get a tattoo if all of their friends had one.
- (**3**) …… said that they would wear uncomfortable shoes if they were trendy.
- (**4**) …… of the class said that they would go out with someone if they were badly dressed.
- (**5**) …… said that they would always buy designer-label clothes if they had the money.
- (**6**) …… said that they would be embarrassed if their mum or dad had a pierced tongue.

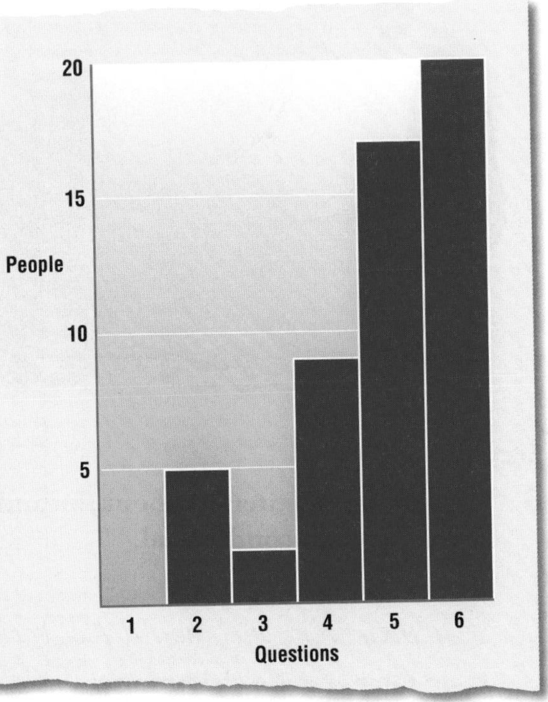

5 **Write a report. Use your class results from exercise 3.**

Our class did the fashion victims questionnaire. Nobody said that …

Finished?

Illustrate your report with a graph.

Progress Check 4

Body art

1 Put the letters in the correct order.

notcact nessel – *contact lenses*

1 shylatire
2 lejelwyer
3 kame-pu
4 otatot
5 gripnice
6 giw

Describing clothes: adjectives

2 Look at the picture. Which adjectives describe Jim and Ann's clothes?

comfortable – Jim

1 tight
2 dark
3 scruffy
4 bright
5 uncomfortable
6 fashionable

Second conditional

3 Complete the sentences about Jim and Ann. Use the second conditional.

went out / feel better

If they went out, they'd feel better.

1 do some exercise / be stronger
2 wear smarter clothes / be more attractive
3 talk to each other / feel happier
4 eat better food / feel healthier
5 not watch TV / have more time

Third conditional

4 Rewrite the sentences. Use the third conditional.

Colin got an earring because his girlfriend suggested it.

Colin wouldn't have got an earring if his girlfriend hadn't suggested it.

1 Colin met Dawn because a friend invited them to a party.
2 Dawn wasn't happy with her hairstyle so she changed it.
3 Spike wanted a tattoo because his friend had one.
4 Spike liked Stella so he asked her out.
5 Stella didn't go out with Spike because she didn't like his hair.

too, *so* and *such*

5 Choose the correct word for each sentence.

1 Piercing isn't **so** / **such** a good idea.
2 Her hairstyle is **too** / **such** old-fashioned.
3 Contact lenses are **so** / **such** a good invention.
4 Her tattoos are **so** / **such** incredible!
5 Those trousers were **such** / **too** expensive.

The World of English 2

Round-up 2 (page 44)

Revision: **Future forms, first, second and third conditionals, *too*, *so*, *such***

Function: **Ordering in a café**

1 What does Kim order?

Culture File (page 46)

Topic: **Teenagers and the law**

Vocabulary: **The law: nouns and verbs**

2 At what age can you drive a car in Britain and the USA?

The Story of Pop (page 48)

Artist: **The Clash**

Type of music: **Punk**

Song: **I fought the law**

3 When did The Clash form?

Round-up 2

Future forms

1 Choose the correct verb form.

Diane: Hey, have you heard about the demonstration against the new road?

David: Yes, and I (**1**) *go / 'm going to* join it. What about you?

Diane: Yes, I'm going to go, too, with Angela. Where (**2**) *are you meeting / do you meet?*

David: We (**3**) *meet / 're meeting* at the park.

Diane: What time (**4**) *will the demonstration start / does the demonstration start?*

David: It (**5**) *starts / is starting* at half past six and it (**6**) *is finishing / finishes* at 7 p.m.

Diane: Do you think there (**7**) *are / will be* a lot of people?

David: Yes, I'm sure there will. We don't need a new road and we don't want them to cut down the trees in the park. Where (**8**) *will our children play / are our children playing?*

Diane: A good question!

First conditional

2 Complete the sentences. Use the first conditional.

Help the world

- If you (**1**) .... (buy) things from our charity, we (**2**) .... (help) people live better lives.
- If we (**3**) .... (make) more money, we (**4**) .... (build) a school for poor children.
- If children (**5**) .... (go) to school, they (**6**) .... (get) a better education.
- If they (**7**) .... (be) educated, they (**8**) .... (not have to) work in poorly paid jobs, and some (**9**) .... (start) their own businesses.
- If they (**10**) .... (run) their own businesses they (**11**) .... (employ) people.
- If they (**12**) .... (pay) people fairly everyone (**13**) .... (become) richer.

Second and third conditional

3 Complete the text. Use the second and third conditional tenses.

If you had an interview tomorrow what would you wear? (**1**) .... you .... (put on) normal clothes or a smart suit or dress? What other changes (**2**) .... you .... (make)? For example, (**3**) .... you .... (take out) your pierced jewellery?

Julia Goodall thinks she got a job as a hotel receptionist because she was the best-dressed person at the interview. 'I'm sure they (**4**) .... (not give) me the job if I (**5**) .... (dress) in scruffy clothes. They (**6**) .... (chose) someone who was clean and smart.'

However, you can sometimes be too smart. If you (**7**) .... (go) to an interview for a job building houses, the bosses (**8**) .... (be) surprised if you (**9**) .... (arrive) in a beautiful suit. The points to remember are: be clean and smart but dress for the job.

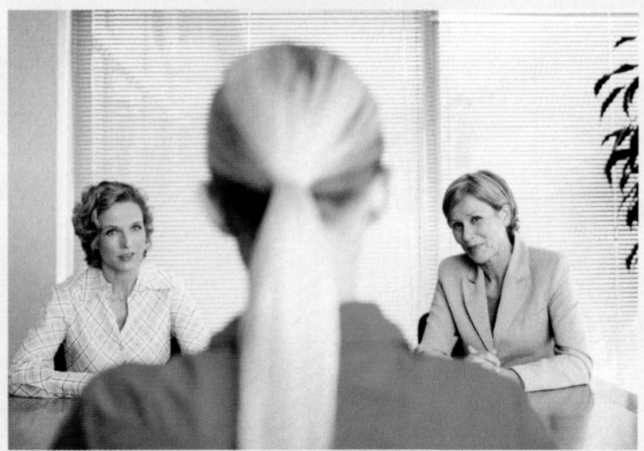

So, such and *too*

4 Complete the text about Tom's day with *so, such* and *too*.

Yesterday, was my first day at my new job and I had (**1**) .... a bad day. I've got tattoos on my arms and I wore a T-shirt. My boss was (**2**) .... angry. She didn't want people to see my tattoos. Then, I broke the computer in the office so I wrote with a pen. I felt (**3**) .... stupid! In the afternoon I was (**4**) .... late for a meeting. After (**5**) .... a bad start I hope today will be better!

Listening

Ordering in a café

1 Complete the dialogue with words in the box. Then listen and check.

your change
Here you are
That's ...
Anything else?
How much is that?
I think I'll have chocolate cake
What type of cake would you like?
What can I get you?

Kim: Good morning.
Waiter: Good morning. **(1)** ....
Kim: I'll have a coffee with milk, please.
Waiter: **(2)** ....
Kim: Yes, a piece of cake.
Waiter: **(3)** ....
Kim: What have you got?
Waiter: Well, there's carrot cake, chocolate cake, cream cake and fruit cake.
Kim: **(4)** ...., please.
Waiter: **(5)** ....
Kim: Oh, I'm sorry. I've changed my mind. I think I'll have the fruit cake.
Waiter: Of course madam. Here you are. Is that OK?
Kim: Yes, it's fine. **(6)** ....
Waiter: That's one coffee and a piece of fruit cake. **(7)**............ £3.50.
Kim: Here you are.
Waiter: Thank you, and here's **(8)** ....

Useful expressions

2 Find the expressions in the dialogue. What do they mean?

1 What can I get you?
2 Anything else?
3 I've changed my mind.
4 Here's your change.

3 Make a list of things you can order in a café.

1 milkshake

Menu

Hot food

....
....
....

Sandwiches

cheese and tomato
....
....

Desert and cakes

carrot cake
....
....

Hot drinks

....
....
....
....

Cold drinks

milkshake
....
....
....

Dialogue

Ordering in a café

4 In pairs, discuss your ideas from exercise 3. Use the dialogue below as a model. Substitute the blue words to form your own dialogues.

A: Can I have another cappuccino, please?

B: Anything else?

A: Yes, I'll have a piece of carrot cake, please.

B: Here you are. That'll be £3.20, please. Thank you.

A: Thanks very much.

Culture File 2

Teenagers and the law

1 Read the text. Then answer the questions.

In Britain, at what age can you:

1. leave school?
2. work more than two hours on a school day?
3. marry with your parents' consent?
4. leave home without permission?
5. buy a dog?
6. go into a pub or bar?

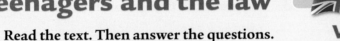

Vocabulary

The law: nouns and verbs

2 Complete the table with words from the text.

noun	verb
permission	permit
(1)	punish
ban	(2) ......
marriage	(3) ......
prosecution	(4) ......
voter	(5) ......

3 Work in pairs. Discuss the questions.

1. Do you think the laws in Britain are fair?
2. Are the laws in your country stricter than the laws in Britain?
3. What is legal and illegal for people of your age?

Teenagers and the law

School

School is obligatory in Britain until the age of sixteen. Police can prosecute parents if their children are absent from school without a good reason.

Work

You can work when you are thirteen years old, but you mustn't work more than two hours on a school day. You can work full time at the age of sixteen.

Punishment

Adults are not allowed to use physical violence against young people in schools. In Britain, corporal punishment was banned from state schools in 1986 and from private schools in 1988.

Marriage

When you are eighteen you are allowed to leave home or get married without your parents' consent. You can get married or leave home from the age of sixteen, but you must have their permission. If your parents don't give permission to marry, you can present your case in court.

Tattoos

It is illegal to tattoo a person who is under eighteen.

NO ALCOHOL TO UNDER 18s - IT'S THE LAW!

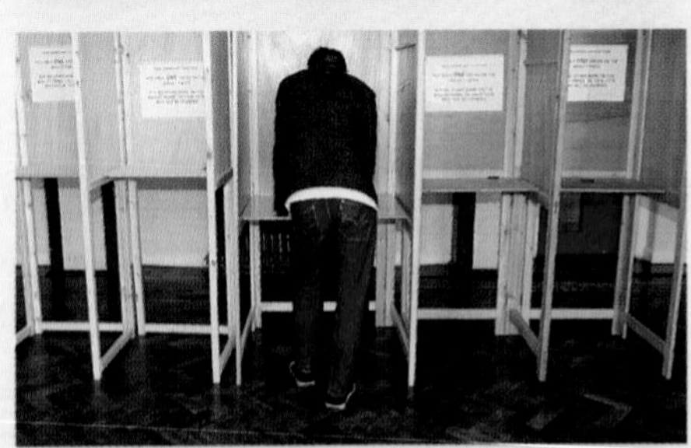

IT IS ILLEGAL TO SELL TOBACCO PRODUCTS TO ANYONE UNDER THE AGE OF 16.

Animals

If you are under twelve you aren't allowed to buy a pet without your parents' consent.

Cigarettes and alcohol

If you are under eighteen you can go to a bar or pub if you are with an adult, but you must leave before nine p.m. You can't buy alcohol until you are eighteen. In Britain you aren't allowed to smoke or buy cigarettes if you are under sixteen.

Films and games

Some videos, DVDs and computer games cannot be bought by people under twelve and many others can only be sold to people who are over eighteen. Cinemas do not allow teenagers to see a film if they are too young.

Voting

You can vote when you are eighteen years old.

Driving

You can learn to drive a car or motorbike from the age of seventeen. You can ride a moped when you're sixteen.

4 **Look at the pictures. What ages do you think people have to be to do these things in the USA? Match the ages to the pictures.**

a 14–18 years old **c** 13–21 years old

b 18 years old

1 vote

2 get married

Did you know?

In the USA:

- children must go to school until they are 16.
- the minimum age when people can work is 14.
- physical punishment is allowed in schools.
- the law about tattoos varies from state to state – some states have no minimum age.

3 drive

5 **Listen and check your answers.**

6 **Listen again and answer the questions.**

1 What could the voting age change to in California in the future?
2 Are all the marriage laws the same for males and females?
3 Can 14 year-olds drive alone in South Dakota?
4 How many cities have curfews for teenagers?
5 When are young people not allowed in the streets in Austin, Texas?

Project

Design an advertising poster to campaign for a change to a law in your country.

- Choose a law.
- Explain why you want to change it.
- Explain what you want to change it to.
- Design the poster.
- Use photos or drawings in your design.

Show your poster to the other groups and vote to choose the best one.

The Story of Pop 2

Punk

1 Read and listen. Then answer the questions.

1. What were the differences between punk bands and supergroups?
2. What was the image of punk rockers?
3. When did The Clash form?
4. Why were some of The Clash's concerts banned?
5. What happened to The Clash after the punk era?

2 Complete the song with a–h. Then listen and check.

a feels so bad
b feels so bad
c ever had
d ever had
e hot sun
f lost my fun
g a six gun
h I had none

Punk

Punk rock started in the 1970s, with an explosion of new bands in the USA and Britain. The young people who started these bands were bored with supergroups, disco music, and the music industry in general. They were also bored with society and its fashions. Punk music was aggressive. The music and the image of punk rockers was the opposite of the '70s supergroups. They played short, angry songs in small auditoriums with basic equipment. Their hair, clothes and music were shocking.

The Clash

The Clash formed in 1976, a year when many musicians were influenced by the anarchy and the energy of Britain's first punk band, The Sex Pistols.

Later, when The Clash and The Sex Pistols went on tour together, a lot of their concerts were banned because the authorities were worried about violence.

The Clash were rebels. A lot of their early songs were anti-government or anti-law. Commercially, they were very successful. When the punk era ended, The Clash continued and their music evolved into different styles.

I fought the law

Breaking rocks in the (**1**) …… .
I fought the law and the law won. (*x2*)

I needed money 'cause (**2**) …… .
I fought the law and the law won. (*x2*)

I left my baby and it (**3**) …… .
Guess my race is run.
She's the best girl that I (**4**) …… .
I fought the law and the law won. (*x2*)

Robbing people with (**5**) …… .
I lost my girl and I (**6**) …… .
I fought the law and the law won. (*x2*)

I left my baby and it (**7**) …… .
Guess my race is run.
She's the best girl that I (**8**) …… .
I fought the law and the law won.
I fought the law and the …
I fought the law and the law won. (*x11*)

Glossary
'cause = because
(I) guess = I suppose
my baby = my girlfriend

Art world

Have a look!

Find the pages where you:

- **read about graffiti artists.**
- **write the biography of an artist.**
- **listen to people identifying a mystery artist.**

Vocabulary

Describing art: adjectives

1 Check the meaning of the words in the box. Then listen and repeat.

contemporary simple beautiful
realistic modern expressive fun
depressing shocking sophisticated

VOCABULARY PAGE 127, 5.1

1 Gauguin – *Women of Tahiti*

3 Van Gogh – *Starry Night over the Rhone*

Speaking

2 Give your opinion about the pictures. Use adjectives from exercise 1.

I like picture 1. I think it's ...

2 Velázquez – *The Spinners*

4 Leonardo da Vinci – *Mona Lisa*

5 Picasso – *Weeping Woman*

5a Masterpieces

Listening

1 Read Jane's diary and look at the photo. Who is with Jane?

We moved into the house today, and my father found an old painting on top of a very old piece of furniture in the attic. We don't know much about art, but my brother Paul and I have decided to take the painting to our art teacher. Who knows – perhaps the painting was the work of a famous artist!

2 Compare Jane's mystery picture with the pictures on page 49. Guess which artist painted the mystery picture. Choose a name from the box.

I think that the artist was ...

Picasso   Leonardo da Vinci   Velázquez   Gauguin   Van Gogh

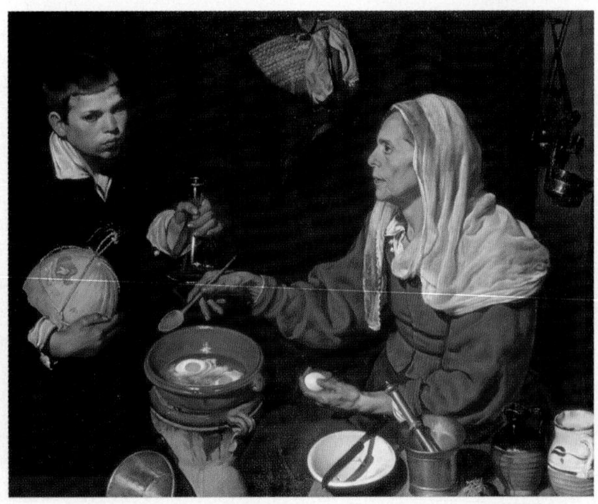

3 Listen to Jane, Paul and Ms Wilkinson. Answer the questions.

1 In what order do they mention the artists from exercise 2?

2 Who painted the mystery picture?

4 Complete Jane's notes with the words in the box. Then listen again and check your answers.

Van Gogh   ~~brighter~~   original   Velázquez   Leonardo   modern   important

Colour

Gauguin's colours are *brighter*.

Paul thought that the artist might be (**1**) ...... because the colours are similar.

Subject

Leonardo painted religious pictures and rich or (**2**) ...... people.

Technique

(**3**)...... used more paint than our artist.

Style

Our painting can't be Picasso's work. Picasso's style was more (**4**)....... .

Conclusion

Ms Wilkinson thinks the artist may be (**5**)...... because the colours and the subject are similar.

Ms Wilkinson says that our painting must be a copy because the (**6**)...... painting is in a gallery.

Exploring grammar

Possibility: *may / might*, *must* and *can't*

5 Look at the examples. Then complete the rules with *may*, *might*, *must*, *can't* and infinitive.

Possibly

We **might** have a famous painting.
It **may** be his work.

Definitely

Your picture **must** be a copy.
Leonardo **can't** be your painter.

Rules

1 When we are sure about something we use (1) ...... and (2) ....
2 When we are not sure about something we use (3) ...... and (4) ....
3 After a modal verb we use an (5) ....

GRAMMAR ▶ PAGES 118–119

6 Look at Danny's picture. Choose the correct words in the sentences.

Danny (**must**) / **can't** be at primary school.

1 He **might** / **can't** be an artist in the future.
2 He **must** / **can't** like trees.
3 He **might** / **can't** be very old.
4 Danny's teacher **must** / **can't** be happy with the picture.
5 Danny **can't** / **might** have artistic parents.
6 The family **may** / **must** live in the city.

7 Read the newspaper report. Then complete the sentences with *might*, *must* and *can't*.

$ million pictures stolen from artist's house

Police are investigating a mysterious robbery of two paintings worth millions of dollars from the home of artist Bianca Brown. The police found no clues at the scene of the robbery, and the thief did not break any windows or doors to enter the house. However, a neighbour saw a man run very fast from the house to a car in which another person was waiting.
'I am very sad. The thief took the two best paintings in the house,' said Ms Brown.

The thief *might* be very rich now.

1 The thief ...... have a key to the house.
2 He ...... be an expert criminal.
3 He ...... be very old.
4 He ...... work alone.
5 He ...... know about art.

Speaking

8 Work in pairs. Exchange opinions about the robbery. Explain your opinions.

The thief might be very rich now, because the paintings were valuable.

Vocabulary

Art: nouns

9 Guess the meanings of the words in the box. Then check in a dictionary.

mural abstract gallery nude portrait
exhibition sculpture still life landscape

VOCABULARY ▶ PAGE 127, 5.2

Finished?

Write definitions for the words in exercise 9. Test your partner.

This is often a picture of a person's face. (portrait)

5b Art or crime?

Reading

Mart and Sandy are teenagers from San Francisco in the USA. They are talking about graffiti in an interview for a magazine.

1 Read the interview. Match questions 1–5 with answers a–e.

Art or crime?

1. **What exactly are you doing here?**
2. **Why do you like the work on this project?**
3. **You mentioned 'taggers'. Can you explain some of the words and expressions that graffiti artists use?**
4. **Why do people do graffiti?**
5. **Do you think that graffiti is an art or a crime?**

a Yeah, sure. 'Tagging' means painting graffiti. In the past 'tag' meant someone's name, but now any graffiti can be called a 'tag'. A good piece of work is a 'burner' and a new or inexperienced artist is called a 'toy'. Some people work in teams called 'crews'. And we talk about a 'tag war' when different people are trying to mark the same territory. OK?

b Well, people want to express themselves, but it's also exciting, you know, because the police can arrest you and give you a fine or put you in prison, so there's a risk. Some crews use walkie-talkies. There's a physical danger too – some people use climbing equipment if they want to tag a difficult place. It's crazy!

c Good question. I think that it depends where it is and what it is. A good tag can improve an ugly place, but a lot of graffiti is vandalism, you know. It's depressing when you see an ugly name twenty times in the same neighbourhood. Your tag has to look good.

d We're working! The city council is paying us to paint a mural here. There are sixteen teenagers working on this project. Some are volunteers, but some of us were taggers before. The police gave our names to the council and now we're here. It's a good idea. Now we can paint legally.

e Well, when I did tags I had to work a lot at night and I was always worried. I couldn't paint in public. But this is great! I can work with other teenagers, and the public stop and look at our work. Today some people said that they liked it – they could see that we were doing something positive.

2 Complete the summary of the article. Use six words or phrases from the box.

landscape	'tag war'	volunteers	money	risk	mural	public	police

The council's new project is a (**1**) .... The artists are (**2**) ...... , or they were sent here by the (**3**) .... Some 'tag' artists say that the project is a good idea. They're happy because the (**4**) ...... like it, although there isn't much (**5**) ...... for the artists on the project. Some graffiti can be really ugly, for example when there is a (**6**) ...... in a district, but the mural is different – it's artistic.

Exploring grammar

Ability and obligation: *can* / *could* and *have to* / *had to*

3 Complete the table and answer the questions.

	Affirmative	Negative
Present	(1)	can't
Past	could	(2) ......
Present	have to (3)	don't have to doesn't have to
Past	(4)	didn't have to

1 Which verb forms its negative with *do* or *did*?
2 What is the negative form of *can*?
3 What is the past form of *can*?

GRAMMAR PAGE 119

4 Choose the correct words.

Graffiti cleaners

It's great that we **can** / **can't** clean the graffiti in this district now. We've got 42 students on our 'Graffiti Cleaners' project. They're volunteers – they (1) **don't have to** / **have to** help, but they want a clean city. Before the project started we (2) **can't** / **couldn't** work very fast. We cleaned a wall and then we (3) **have to** / **had to** clean it again a week later. Now we (4) **can** / **had to** send people immediately.

(Eva González – Police officer)

In my opinion young people (5) **don't have to** / **have to** try to improve this area. We (6) **don't have to** / **didn't have to** think about this problem before, but there are a lot of gangs here now. I'm happy that I (7) **can** / **couldn't** help.

(Sam Jones – Student)

5 Complete the text with the words in the box.

don't can find have to wear use ~~couldn't paint~~ had to learn couldn't do

I *couldn't paint* when I was younger but I was always interested in art. At school we usually had to (**1**) ...... traditional materials, but now I always work with metal.

I (**2**) ...... to use the equipment. At first I (**3**) ...... a straight line, but I've done three courses now and I make some nice things.

I enjoy it, but it isn't easy and you (**4**) ...... protective clothes. I (**5**) ...... old metal in a lot of places, so usually I (**6**) ...... have to pay for my materials.

Pronunciation

Recognizing contractions

6 Listen to the sentences. Do you hear verb a or b in each sentence?

	a		b	
1	**a**	can	**b**	can't
2	**a**	could	**b**	couldn't
3	**a**	didn't	**b**	couldn't
4	**a**	don't	**b**	can't

7 Listen again and write the sentences.

Finished?

Look at the letters in the words on the wall. Make more words with the letters.

sit, far, ...

GRAFFITI ARTIST

5c Reaction

Speaking

1 Work in pairs. Look at the pieces of modern art and the opinions about them. Do you agree with the opinions?

A: Do you agree with opinion 1?

B: No, I don't. I think it's an interesting piece of art.

1 'A dead shark? It's horrible. This might offend some people.'

2 'This isn't art, it's just a box. Art has to be beautiful.'

3 'What is it? This artist can't paint and the picture has got no meaning.'

4 'It's a bed – and it isn't even clean! This must be a joke – it's not serious.'

Listening

2 Listen to a programme about reactions to modern art. In what order does the programme mention works 1–4?

3 Work in pairs. Complete the notes with a–j. Then listen again and check your answers.

1 c

Artist	Year of exhibition	Reactions
(1) *Duchamp*	1913	(2) ......
(3)	(4)	'Any object could be art.' (5) ......
(6)	1997	(7) ...... People threw eggs and paint at a picture.
(8)	(9)	(10) ...... A collector bought it for $334,000.

a Hirst
b Emin
c ~~Duchamp~~
d Warhol

e 1999
f 1964

g 'It wasn't artistic.'
h 'It was the end of art history.'
i People broke windows at the gallery.
j Students painted their bodies and jumped on it.

Writing

Biography of an artist: editing a text

You should check and improve a text before you write a final version.

4 Read the student's biography of Andy Warhol. Then look at the teacher's checklist. Match 1–5 in the checklist with sentences a–e in the text.

Editing your work – checklist

1 Do you think that a reader might want more information about this?
2 Is the information in the correct order?
3 Is this information really necessary?
4 Do you repeat this information?
5 Is the grammar, punctuation and spelling correct?

Andy Warhol

Andy Warhol was born in the United States between 1927 and 1930. The exact date of his birth isn't clear. He studied at an Institute of Technology. (a) After that he had worked in New York for magazines and an advertiseing agency. (b) That type of work must be very interesting, I think.

Andy Warhol wasn't a snob. He thought that normal objects could be pieces of art, so he used popular images and objects in his paintings. One critic called this type of art 'Pop art'. Warhol also wanted to make money from his art. The name of his studio was 'The Factory' because he produced a lot of work there.

His work at The Factory made Warhol rich and famous, but he was also interested in cinematic art. He made some very long films in the sixties. One of them was an eight-hour film of a person sleeping. Another film was twenty-five hours long. (c) Andy Warhol started painting in the fifties.

(d) In 1968 a woman shot Warhol. He died in 1987 after an operation in hospital. Some people think that he never really recovered from the attempt to assassinate him. (e) He was very rich and famous when he died in 1987.

5 Read the sentences. Should the student include this information in the biography? Write *Yes* or *No* for each sentence.

1 Warhol's mother's name was Julia.
2 For example, he painted pictures of soup cans and famous drinks bottles.
3 Warhol wanted to sell, sell, sell.
4 I think that 25 hours is too long for a film.
5 She shot him because he ignored her. She wanted to be in one of his films.

6 Write a biography of an artist.

- Find information about an artist.
- Write your first version of the biography.
- Edit your work. Use the checklist in exercise 4.
- Write a final version.

Finished?

Write about four pieces of art from this unit. Describe them and give your opinion.
This is an abstract picture ...

Progress Check 5

Describing art: adjectives

1 Write adjectives for sentences 1–5.

This seems real.

realistic

1 It shocks people.
2 It's by a 21st-century artist.
3 It isn't sophisticated; it's ...
4 It has great beauty.
5 We can see what the artist wants to express.

Art: nouns

2 Identify the types of art in these details from pictures. Use the words in the box.

portrait landscape nude sculpture abstract still life

1

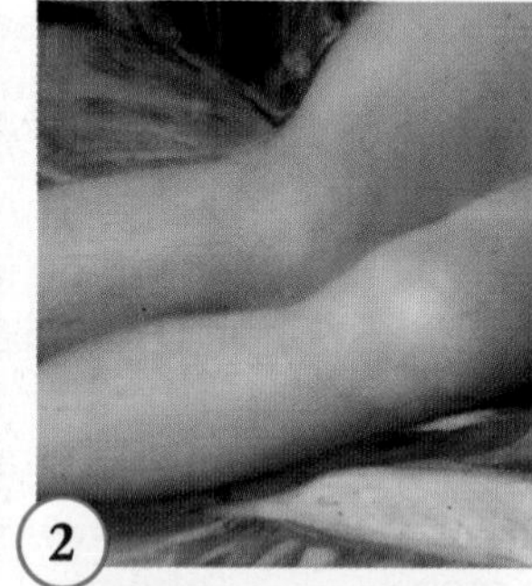

2

3

4

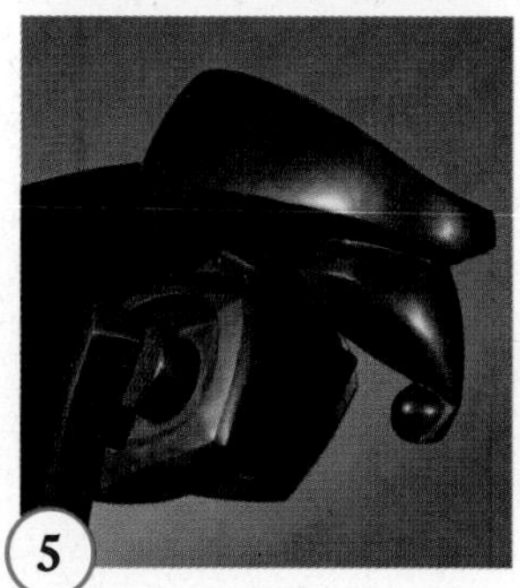

5

6

Possibility: *may / might, must* and *can't*

3 Look at the picture. Then match sentence halves 1–5 with a–e.

1 The sculpture — a ... can't be interested.
2 The attendant — b ... might be surprised.
3 The cleaner — c ... must be 2,000 years old.
4 She — d ... must know about art.
5 The people — e ... might be an artist.

Ability and obligation: *can / could* and *have to / had to*

4 Complete the text with the words in the box.

have to ~~can~~ couldn't had to can't couldn't

Vincent Van Gogh

We *can* admire Van Gogh's work in galleries, but most people (**1**) ...... buy his work. Collectors (**2**) ...... pay millions of dollars for a Van Gogh painting.

But Van Gogh (**3**) ...... sell his work when he was alive. He only sold one painting, so he was very poor. He always (**4**) ...... ask his friends and family for money.

The painter also had health problems and he (**5**) ...... control his emotions: he cut off his ear after a terrible argument with his friend, Paul Gauguin. Van Gogh committed suicide in 1890.

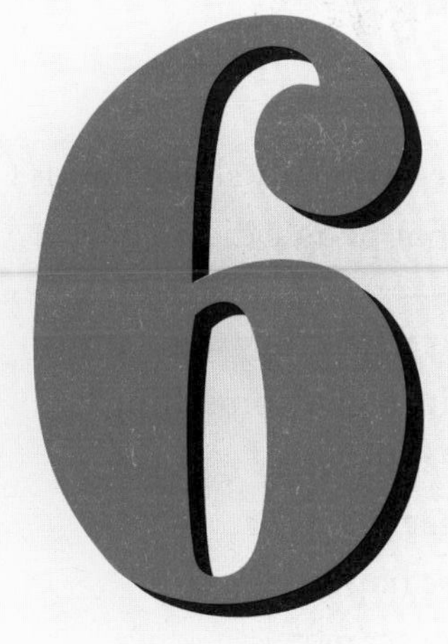

Behaviour

Have a look!

Find the pages where you:

- **do a questionnaire.**
- **read about our behaviour.**
- **listen to a programme about people's good and bad habits.**

Vocabulary

Body language

1 Match pictures 1–9 with the verbs in the box. Then listen and repeat.

smile cry point ~~blush~~ kiss hug shake hands sneer stare

1 blush

VOCABULARY PAGE 127, 6.1

Speaking

2 Talk about the pictures. Describe the people's body language and personalities. Use the words in the box.

confident ~~friendly~~ happy moody quiet sad shy unfriendly

A: The girl in the green T-shirt is smiling.
B: She looks very friendly.

1

2

3

4

5

6

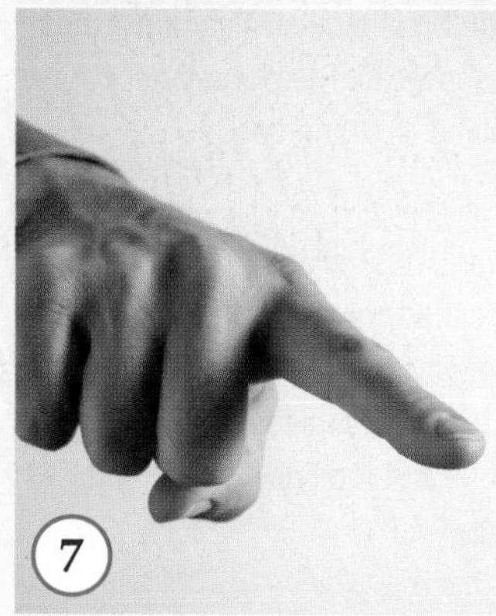
7

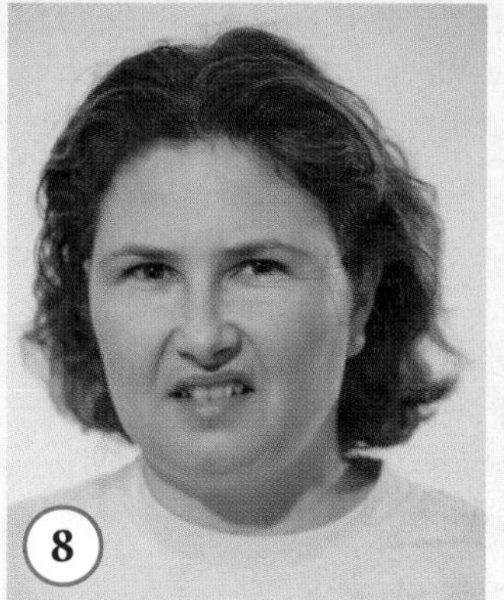
8

9

6a Express yourself

Reading

1 Read and listen. Choose the best title.

a Looking at the past – how did people live and work?
b Animal instincts – how animal behaviour has changed.
c Human behaviour – past and present.

2 Read the text again and answer the questions.

1 What does the text say about crying?
  a Crying isn't useful.
  b Crying could help a baby to survive.
  c Crying is never necessary.
2 Why did mothers chew food for their babies?
  a to show affection
  b to communicate
  c to soften the food for the babies to eat
3 Why did people originally shake hands?
  a It showed that people didn't have a weapon.
  b People did it when they were hunting.
  c People did it to give something to another person.
4 When do we sneer?
  a When we are happy.
  b When we are scared.
  c When we don't like something.
5 How did sneering begin in humans?
  a People sneered at animals.
  b It came from a more aggressive expression.
  c Animals did it, and people copied them.

CRYING

A baby's only form of communication is crying. A baby cries when it is hungry or uncomfortable. When we can speak, crying is not really necessary, but we do it because it is our most basic and natural form of communication. Millions of years ago, crying was an important part of our behaviour: if a baby can call its parents, it has a better chance of survival.

KISSING

When babies start eating food, it must be soft. Today this is done by cooking and liquidizing foods, but before the invention of fire, humans could not prepare baby food in this way. Instead adults used to chew the raw meat and vegetables to make them soft enough for their baby to eat. When it was ready, they passed the food from their mouth to the baby's. Feeding in this way was also a sign of affection and created a bond between mother and child. Therefore some scientists believe that this was probably the origin of kissing, and today we still kiss to show affection.

SHAKING HANDS

Shaking hands is popular in many countries, but what was the origin of this behaviour? One explanation is that in the past people carried weapons to hunt and to defend themselves against their enemies. So, when people met a stranger, they opened their hands to show that they were not carrying a weapon. It was then a friendly action to touch the other person by giving him their hand.

SNEERING

Sometimes when we are angry with somebody or if we dislike something, it is very obvious from the expression on our faces. When we raise a lip and show our teeth, it is called sneering. Animals display similar behaviour. They also show their teeth, but in a more aggressive way than humans. For example, when a wolf does it, it looks as though it is about to bite, and bite hard. It shows its teeth to frighten other animals. Our ancestors may have had more aggressive expressions, but today we often try to hide our true feelings and consequently use less obvious body language

Exploring grammar

Gerunds

A gerund is the *-ing* form of a verb.

3 Complete the sentences from the text. Then complete the rule by circling the correct word.

(1) A baby's only form of communication is ....
(2) Some scientists believe this was the origin of ....
(3) ...... hands is popular in many countries.
(4) When we raise a lip and show our teeth, it is called ....

Rule

When we use an **-ing** form as **an adjective / a noun / an adverb**, we call it a gerund.

GRAMMAR PAGE 120

4 Complete the sentences. Use the gerunds of the words in the box.

show ~~communicate~~ stare kiss
smile shake cry

International body language

Communicating clearly is important, but body language isn't the same in all countries.

1 ...... is often romantic, but in many countries people do it just to say 'Hello'.

2 In many cultures, ... hands is common behaviour when people meet.

3 In Britain, women hug their friends more than men do. ...... their feelings in this way is unusual for men in Britain.

4 Some things are rude in many countries, for example .... Most people think it is aggressive to look at strangers for too long.

5 ...... isn't always a sign of sadness. People around the world cry at weddings because they are happy!

6 One really international expression is .... When you smile, people everywhere will understand your feelings.

Infinitive of purpose

We sometimes use *to* + infinitive to explain **why** we do something. It shows the **purpose** of the action.

5 Find the actions in the text. Write the purpose.

Action	Purpose
chewed food	(1) ......
people kiss	(2) ......
show their teeth	(3) ......

GRAMMAR PAGE 120

6 Put the words in the correct order.

1 for food / gone out / They've / hunt / to
2 look for / a tree / climbed / to / eggs / He's

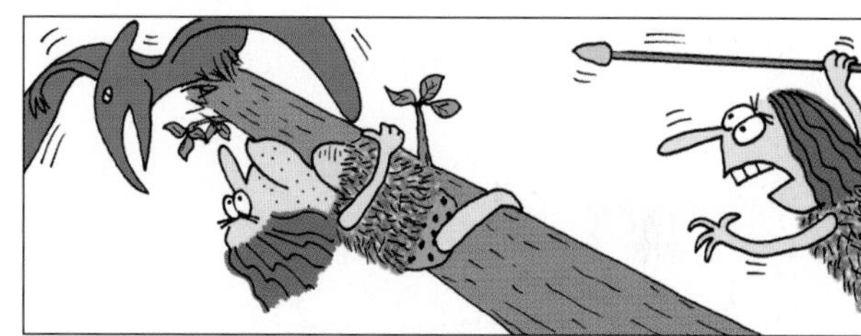

3 to / shouting / the bird / She's / scare
4 using / He's / to / the egg / carry / his shirt

5 a fire / made / cook dinner / to / They've
6 break / using / He's / the egg / a rock / to

Finished?

What is polite or rude in your country?

Polite	Rude
saying hello	*staring at people*

6b Habits

Vocabulary

Describing character: adjectives

1 Write the opposites of the adjectives 1–5. Use *dis-*, *im-* or *un-*. Then listen and check.

polite *impolite*

1 patient ......
2 honest ......
3 romantic ......
4 emotional ......
5 kind ......

VOCABULARY PAGES 127–128, 6.2

Listening

2 Read the text quickly and answer the questions.

1 Where is the text from?
2 Which programmes are about true life and which are fictional?
3 What is the name of the soap opera?
4 What is the relationship between the people in *Confess!*?
5 Which programme has a detective as the star?

3 Look at the photo and guess the person in sentences 1–5. Write *Susan* or *Andy*, then listen and check your answers.

1 ...... is good at maths.
2 ...... uses the phone a lot.
3 ...... complains about untidiness.
4 ...... cleans the house.
5 ...... doesn't tidy up the house.

4 Listen again and answer the questions.

1 How late does Andy stay in bed?
2 Why doesn't Andy mind helping his sister's friends?
3 Why does Andy criticize his girlfriend?
4 What does Susan love doing?
5 What does Susan spend her money on?
6 What is Susan good at?
7 Where does Andy leave his things?
8 How can Susan teach Andy to be tidy?

TV1

7.00 **Albert Street** (soap opera) Jo finds Paul has a guilty secret.

7.30 **Confess!** This week Confess! asks about people's habits. Two of the guests are brother and sister, Andy and Susan Webster. Find out what they said about their family, their friends, themselves and each other!

8.00 **Death on the Nile** (film) A rich heiress is killed on board a boat on the Nile. Can Hercule Poirot solve the case?

10.00 **World news and weather**

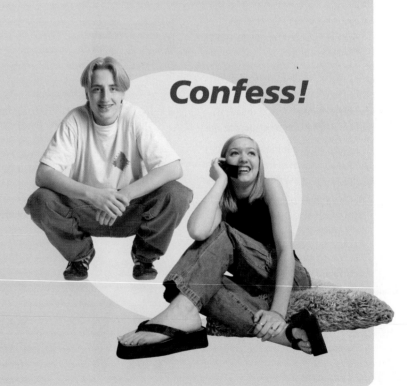

Confess!

Exploring grammar

Gerunds and infinitives

We use gerunds after some verbs, but we use infinitives after others.

5 Look at the examples. Then complete the rules.

I **like sitting** in bed and **watching** TV.
I **love staying** in bed all morning.
My girlfriend **promises to do** things.
He never **tries to help**.
I **hate seeing** the house untidy.
Then he might **agree to tidy up**.

Rules

1 We use **gerunds / infinitives** after verbs of preference, for example: **like, love, enjoy, don't mind** and **hate**.
2 We use **gerunds / infinitives** after verbs of intention, for example: **promise, plan, agree, want** and **try**.

GRAMMAR PAGE 120

6 Complete the dialogue. Use gerunds and infinitives.

Mum: What time will your game finish?
Rick: About seven o'clock, but the others are planning *to go* to the disco after the game. I agreed (**1**) ...... (go) with them.
Mum: Great! I loved (**2**) ...... (dance) when I was your age. I was good, too.
Rick: I know. I remember when you tried (**3**) ...... (teach) me rock 'n' roll. It's really hard!
Mum: You were good! Anyway Rick, please don't stay out late. You know I worry.
Rick: OK, I promise (**4**) ...... (leave) before the end.
Mum: Do you want (**5**) ...... (phone) me? I'll bring the car.
Rick: No, thanks. I like (**6**) ...... (get) the bus with my friends.
Mum: I don't mind (**7**) ...... (take) them home too. I enjoy (**8**) ...... (meet) your table tennis friends.
Rick: Mum, it's football tonight. There are eleven of us!

7 Complete the sentences about you. Use gerunds and infinitives.

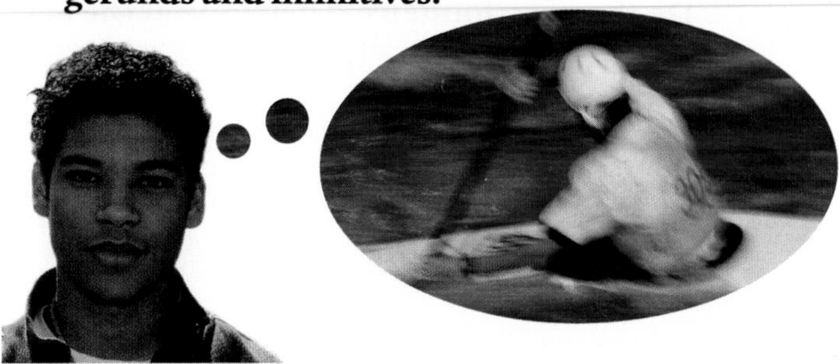

I'm planning to go canoeing at the weekend.

1 I'm planning ...
2 I don't like ...
3 I want ...
4 I like ...
5 I've promised ...
6 I hate ...

Pronunciation

Moving stress

8 Listen and underline the main stress in the blue sentences. Listen again and repeat.

1 **A:** Do you like staying in bed late?
B: Yes! Do you like staying in bed late?

2 **C:** What do you hate doing?
D: Tidying my room. What do you hate doing?

3 **E:** What do you want to do?
F: Watch TV. What do you want to do?

4 **G:** What are you planning to do?
H: Go to the cinema. What are you planning to do?

Speaking

9 Work in pairs. Ask and answer the questions in exercise 8. Remember the moving stress.

Finished?

Look at the adjectives in exercise 1. Then imagine you know one of the people on page 57 and write a description of them.
The person in photo 1 is patient. She doesn't mind waiting.

6c Emotions

Reading

1 Do the questionnaire. Then look at the key.

Speaking

2 Work in pairs. Ask and answer the questions in the questionnaire.

The Emotions Questionnaire

Check your emotional temperature.

Love

1 You're sitting next to the person of your dreams. He or she is talking about romantic things. It's your big chance. What do you do?

a I blush and tell the person that I like them.

b I change the subject.

Happiness

4 You're watching the match on TV and your team scores a goal. What do you do?

a I shout and jump out of my seat.

b I smile for a second, and then I watch the rest of the match.

Anger

2 You're watching a video and there's a lot of violence in the film. What do you do?

a I feel angry and I don't watch the rest of the video.

b I watch the rest of the video. What's the problem? Violence is a part of life.

Jealousy

5 You're sitting in a café and you see your ex-boyfriend or ex-girlfriend with a new partner. They're kissing. What do you do?

a I stare at them. I really want to shout at them.

b I avoid eye contact and I try not to think about them.

Sadness

3 You're watching a very sad film. Do you cry?

a Probably, I don't think that crying is a bad thing.

b Probably not, I don't usually cry.

Fear

6 You're walking down a dark street at night. You hear noises behind you. A person is following you. What do you do?

a I feel scared. I start to walk faster, and then I turn round and look at the person.

b I don't turn round or walk faster. I don't want to show fear.

Key

Mostly *a* answers: You're a sensitive person and things affect you a lot. Your emotions are strong, and sometimes you are hot-blooded. That's OK, but be careful; a little control is sometimes a good thing!

Equal number of *a* and *b* answers: You aren't hot-blooded or cold-blooded! You're very balanced. You can control your emotions when necessary, but you can also be expressive.

Mostly *b* answers: You're a cold fish! Have you really got a cold heart, or are you just controlling your emotions? Doctors say that hiding our emotions can cause stress. Remember that laughing and crying are good for you!

Writing

Linking words and giving opinions

3 Read Hilary's emotional profile and find nine more linking words or phrases.

Love: *so*, ... **Hate:** ...... **Fear:** ......, ...

Happiness: ......, ... **Sadness:** ......, ..., ...

Emotional Profile

Name: Hilary Thomson

Love: I love watching films so I try to go to the cinema every week. For me, romantic films are the best.

Hate: I hate getting bad marks in exams. I always look through all my notes again really carefully so that I'll remember everything.

Happiness: I think that home is the place where I feel the happiest because I like being with my family.

Sadness: I feel sad when I see sad films although I know they aren't real! I also feel sad when I'm alone. On the other hand, it gives me time to think.

Fear: Horror films scare me the most, especially when I watch with my brother. He turns the light off and makes silly noises during the film. He always laughs, but I don't think it's funny.

4 Complete the table with the words or phrases from exercise 3. In pairs, translate them into your language.

give reasons or results	contrast information
so	....
connect information	**give opinions**
....	....

5 Choose the correct linking word or phrase.

I hate it when I cry **although** / **because** it's really embarrassing. (**1**) **On the other hand** / **So** you sometimes feel better after. I don't like crying, (**2**) **and** / **but** it's good to cry sometimes.

(**3**) **For me,** / **So that** bad dreams are the worst thing. I often talk in my sleep when I have a bad dream. I (**4**) **also** / **although** shout sometimes. (**5**) **On the other hand,** / **I think that** violent films give people bad dreams.

I'm happy when it rains (**6**) **although** / **so** I don't like getting wet! I love plants and trees (**7**) **but** / **so** I know that rain is a good thing. I like sitting near the window (**8**) **so that** / **although** I can watch the rain.

6 Write your emotional profile. Use the form in exercise 3, Hilary's words in blue and the words from the table in exercise 4.

Study skills

Learning vocabulary: adjectives and nouns

It's good to learn adjectives and nouns in pairs.

7 Copy and complete the table. Use a dictionary to help you.

Adjective	Noun	Adjective	Noun
emotional	emotion	jealous	(**3**) ......
angry	(**1**)	violent	(**4**) ......
(**2**)	sadness	(**5**)	sensitivity

Finished?

Make a list of positive and negative qualities. Use a dictionary to help you.

Positive	*Negative*
kindness	*dishonesty*

Progress Check 6

Body language

1 Put the letters in order. Then translate the verbs.

tesra – *stare*

1 siks	**3** resne	**5** ryc	**7** tiopn
2 slime	**4** ghu	**6** shulb	**8** sahek

Describing character: adjectives

2 Write about Sue. Use the adjectives in the box.

emotional honest kind polite unromantic ~~patient~~

Sue doesn't mind if you arrive late. *She's patient.*

1. She tells the truth.
2. She likes helping people.
3. She always says 'please' and 'thank you'.
4. She doesn't like romantic films.
5. She laughs and cries a lot.

3 Write the opposites of the adjectives in exercise 2.

patient – impatient

4 Complete the factfile with gerunds.

Animal habit factfile: sea lions

Sleeping (sleep) takes up a lot of these animals' time. When they're awake, their behaviour is mainly (**1**) …… (dive) for food and (**2**) …… (fight) about territory. (**3**) …… (spend) time around them can be dangerous, and (**4**) …… (study) them creates difficulties even for experts. (**5**) …… (get) close to them isn't easy, so for most of us, the only way to see them up close is by (**6**) …… (watch) them on TV.

Infinitive of purpose

5 Match the actions and purposes. Then write sentences about Tim's party.

Tim had a party to celebrate his birthday.

What they did: action	Why they did it: purpose.
1 ~~Tim had a party~~	buy a present for him.
2 He phoned all his friends	~~celebrate his birthday.~~
3 He bought a new T-shirt	leave them alone.
4 His girlfriend saved her money	listen to.
5 Everyone brought their favourite CDs	invite them.
6 His parents went out all evening	wear at the party.

Gerunds and infinitives

6 Complete the text with gerunds and infinitives.

Old habits never die

Valentine's Day, February 14th, is the day when millions of people enjoy *receiving* (receive) cards from secret admirers. Most people like (**1**) …… (send) romantic cards, but they don't put their names on them. They want (**2**) …… (keep) their names a secret. Human behaviour is strange! However, there's another tradition in Britain that is even stranger. In the past, women agreed (**3**) …… (become) a man's wife or not, but they never asked the man. It wasn't acceptable – except on one special day, February 29th. It's in fashion again in Britain, so if you're a woman, are you planning (**4**) …… (ask) the man of your dreams? If you're the man, will you promise (**5**) …… (love) her for ever? If this sounds scary, don't worry. February 29th only happens once every four years. You can hide!

The World of English 3

Round-up 3 (page 66)

Revision: Modal verbs of possibility, ability and obligation, gerunds and infinitives

Function: Asking for permission and making requests

1 At what time must Kim be home?

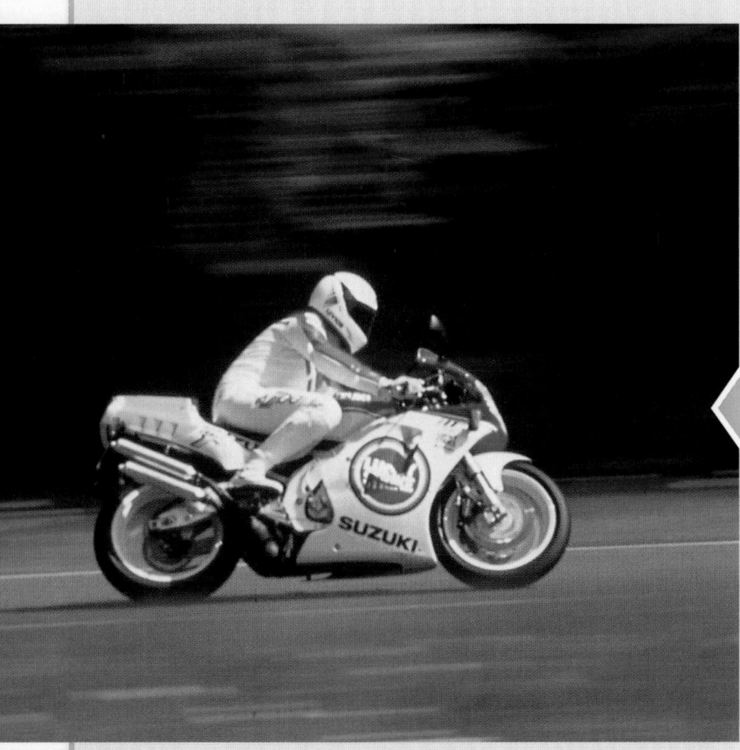

Culture File (page 68)

Topic: On the road

Vocabulary: Driving

2 Is Britain the only country where people drive on the left?

The Story of Pop (page 70)

Artist: Run DMC

Type of music: Hip hop

Song: It's like that

3 Where did hip hop music start?

Round-up 3

Possibility, ability and obligation

1 Choose the correct verbs.

Alice: Hi Kate, are you enjoying New York?
Kate: It's fantastic. I've been to lots of art exhibitions.
Alice: Have you seen the exhibition of Native American art at the Museum of Modern Art?
Kate: It (**1**) *can't / might* be at the MOMA because I went there yesterday.
Alice: Oh, it (**2**) *can't / must* be on at a different art gallery. Well, what did you see?
Kate: I saw a Picasso exhibition but I (**3**) *had to / must* wait an hour before I (**4**) *could / can* go in, and it was snowing!
Alice: And where are you going today?
Kate: Well, this morning I want to visit the Empire State Building. I (**5**) *have to / can* walk there in 15 minutes from the hotel. But it's Sunday so it (**6**) *may / can* be closed.
Alice: Are you going to go to a baseball game?
Kate: I (**7**) *couldn't / had not* get a ticket. I (**8**) *have to / can* do some shopping and I really want to go to the Metropolitan Museum. There are so many things there that I think I (**9**) *might / can't* be there all day!
Alice: And what about visiting the rest of the city?
Kate: Well, in one week you (**10**) *can't / don't have* see all there is to see in New York!
Alice: I'm sure it (**11**) *must / might* be fantastic!
Kate: Well, when I get home we can start planning a trip together!

Gerunds and infinitives

2 Complete the text with the verbs. Use gerunds or infinitives of purpose.

watch listen relax teach practise laugh tell learn

Smiling and (**1**)................ make you feel good. You probably know that, but scientists have shown that they are actually good for our minds and bodies too. Children laugh a lot, but many adults forget how to do it, so they have to have help (**2**) .... them how to laugh again. Doctors know that (**3**) .... a DVD of a television comedy programme and (**4**) .... to CDs of people laughing can help people. The teachers play the programmes and CDs (**5**) .... the students. Then the students have to tell a funny story or a joke about their lives to the others. (**6**) .... the stories and jokes helps the students see that their lives have happy moments. After class there is homework. (**7**) .... what they have done in class is important. Every morning they must stand in front of a mirror and laugh for five minutes. Then they must collect jokes and funny stories for the next class. (**8**) .... to laugh again is a serious business!

3 Complete the text. Use gerunds and infinitives.

Most people enjoy *going* to the cinema, but we don't all like (**1**)................ (see) the same types of films. Some people hate (**2**)................ (look at) violence and others don't mind it. Although that is true, Hollywood film producers try (**3**)................ (produce) films that will be liked by everybody! Film-makers want (**4**)................ (make) a lot of money. That is why producers plan (**5**)................ (have) lots of different emotions in every film. Producers know that most of us love (**6**)................ (watch) stories with lots of romance, anger, sadness, fear, jealousy and happiness.

When a film is nearly finished the producers show it to a group of twenty or thirty people for free if they agree (**7**)................ (answer) a few questions after they have seen it.

Listening

Asking for permission

1 Read the expressions and decide who says them: Kim (*K*) or her mother (*M*). Then listen and check.

1 Is it okay if I go to the disco tonight? K

2 ... you have to be home by 11 o'clock. .....

3 I suppose so. .....

4 Oh, that's not a very good place, is it? .....

5 All my friends from school are going. .....

6 Can I borrow your black t-shirt? .....

7 Is that boy with the motorbike going? .....

8 ... don't go on his motorbike. .....

9 ... could you lend me some money? .....

10 What on earth is that? .....

11 I've been worried sick! .....

12 You're grounded! .....

Useful expressions

2 These expressions were in the dialogue. What do they mean?

1 I suppose so.

2 We were worried sick about you!

3 What on earth is that?

4 You're grounded!

3 Make a list of things that you need to ask permission to do. Use the ideas in the pictures.

1 have a party

SCHOOL TRIP TO LONDON
23–25 March
Chance to see:
Tower Bridge and Tower of London
Science Museum
Hyde Park
British Museum
Houses of Parliament and Big Ben

Dialogue

Asking for and giving permission

4 In pairs, discuss your ideas from exercise 3. Use the dialogue below as a model. Substitute the blue words to form your own dialogues.

A: Mum, is it OK if I go out tonight?

B: Yes, all right, but can you be home before eleven o'clock?

A: Yes, no problem. Could you lend me some money?

B: Oh, Kate! Yes, I suppose so.

A: Thanks, Mum.

Culture File 3

On the road

1 Match the words in the box with pictures 1–6.

driving licence   L-plate   speed camera
speed limit   scooter   motorbike

2 Work with a partner. Discuss sentences 1–6. Are they true or false for your country?

I think number 1 is true.

1 Motorbikes are more popular than scooters.
2 Distances are measured in metres and kilometres.
3 The maximum speed limit is 100 kilometres an hour.
4 You must drive on the left.
5 The most popular motorbikes are Japanese.
6 You can ride a moped when you are fourteen.

3 Look at the sentences in exercise 2 again and read the text. Are the sentences true or false for Britain?

On the road

Bikes

Not many teenagers ride scooters in Britain – motorbikes are more common. The most popular motorbikes are Japanese: Honda, Suzuki and Kawasaki.

Speed

Distances on British roads are measured in miles. A mile is 1.6 kilometres. The maximum speed limit is 70 miles an hour – that's 112.6 kilometres an hour. There are a lot of speed cameras in Britain and it's really not a good idea to break the speed limit.

Learning

When you're sixteen you can ride a moped if you've done a CBT (Compulsory Basic Training) course. Then you must use L-plates until you've passed a motorcycle test, which you can take when you are seventeen.

On the road

Until the end of the 18th century vehicles in all countries travelled on the left side of the road. This changed when the French Emperor Napoleon changed the rules of the road in Europe. Most other governments followed France and now the majority of Europeans drive on the right. In Britain and its colonies people continued to drive on the left and this has never changed. It's sometimes difficult for visitors!

Grand Prix

Motorbike racing is popular in Britain and every year thousands of people go to the British motorcycle Grand Prix in Donnington. It's a fast circuit, and the big 500 cc bikes reach speeds of more than 250 kilometres an hour.

4 **Listen to the conversation between Ellen, from the USA, and Ted, from Britain, about driving in the USA. Which things in photos a–d do they mention?**

a

b

Did you know?

Henry Ford was an American industrialist, who started making cars at the end of the 19th century, when not many people owned cars. His ambition was to produce cars at a price many more people could afford. In 1908, he realized his ambition with his car the model T-Ford. He produced this in large factories where everything was made in one place. By 1927 he had produced 15 million cars and become the richest man in the USA.

c

d

5 **Listen again and complete the table.**

	Britain	USA
cars are usually automatic	*no*	(1) ......
drive on left or right	*left*	(2) ......
laws: same or different across the country	*same*	(3) ......
lights: on or off in the day	(4)	*on in some states*
top speed limit (miles per hour)	*70*	*usually* (5) ......

Project

Make a leaflet for drivers from abroad. Give them advice on driving in your country. Include information about:

- different speed limits
- which side of the road to drive on
- the minimum age to drive
- other important rules
- dangerous roads or parts of the country
- other important information

Use photos, drawings, diagrams or maps.

The Story of Pop 3

Hip hop

1 Read and listen. Then answer the questions.

1 Where was DJ Kool Herc from?
2 Where did rap originate?
3 What is a hip hop 'posse'?
4 When was Run DMC formed and by whom?
5 When did rap music become popular with white people?

Hip hop

Hip hop, like punk, is often a form of social protest. It started in the 1970s in the USA, when a Jamaican, DJ Kool Herc, imported a tradition from his country. While he was playing records, Kool Herc invented rhyming commentaries, which he spoke into a microphone. Other black DJs copied and extended this style, and they called it 'rap'. Hip hop groups or 'posses' consisted of DJs, MCs (Master of Ceremonies), breakdancers and graffiti artists. The DJs played the records, while the MCs provided the raps.

Run DMC

Joseph Simmons and Darryl McDaniels were a rap duo when they were still at high school. In 1982, when they left school, they formed Run DMC with DJ Jason Mizzell.

Run DMC was the first hip hop group on MTV. In 1986, they worked with the heavy metal band Aerosmith, creating a fusion of rock and hip hop. The record, *Walk this way*, was popular with both black and white teenagers, and it was the first hip hop record in the US top 10.

2 Complete the song. Use the words in the box. Then listen and check.

die	prejudiced	feet	play	why	clothes	day	search

It's like that

Unemployment at a record high.
People coming, people going, people born to (**1**) ....
Don't ask me, because I don't know (**2**) ....
But it's like that, and that's the way it is.
People in the world try to make ends meet.
You try to ride car, train, bus, or (**3**) ....
I said you got to work hard to want to compete.
It's like that, and that's the way it is! Huh!

Money is the key to end all your woes.
Your ups, your downs, your highs and your lows.
Won't you tell me last time that love bought
you (**4**) ...... ?
It's like that, and that's the way it is.
Bills fly higher every (**5**) ....
We receive much lower pay.
I'd rather stay young, go out and (**6**) ....
It's like that, and that's the way it is! Huh!

When you feel you fail sometimes it hurts
For a meaning in life is why you (**7**) ....
Take the boys on the train, drive to school or
the church.
It's like that, and that's the way it is.
Here's another point in life you should not miss.
Do not be a fool who's (**8**) ....
Because we're all written down on the same list
It's like that (what?) and that's the way it is! Huh!

(Chorus)
You know it's like that,
and that's the way it is.
Because it's like that,
and that's the way it is.

(Repeat chorus x3)

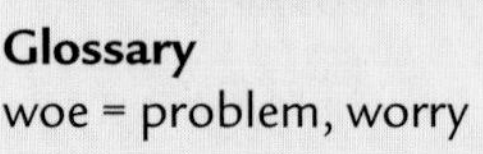

Glossary
woe = problem, worry

Travel

Have a look!

Find the pages where you:

- **write a letter.**
- **read about a man's adventure.**
- **listen to a programme about unusual hotels.**

Vocabulary

Geographical features

1 Match features 1–10 with the words in the box. Then listen and repeat.

pole equator island continent border ocean lake forest desert mountain range

VOCABULARY PAGE 128, 7.1

Speaking

2 In pairs, ask and answer the questions.

1. Can you name two deserts?
2. Which is the biggest island in the world?
3. Can you name two oceans?
4. Which countries have got borders with your country?
5. Which mountain range is Everest in?
6. Which continent is the Amazon rainforest in?

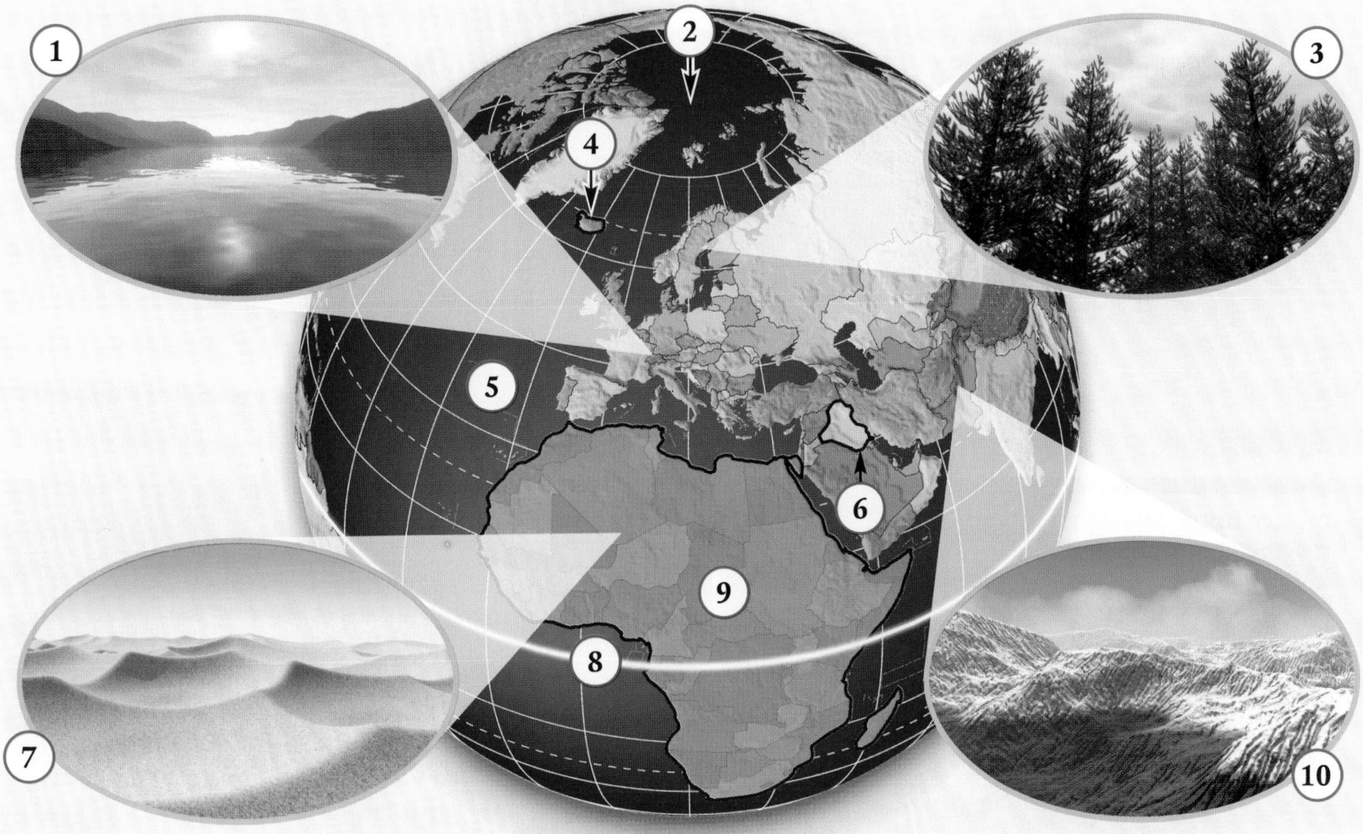

1 2 3 4 5 6 7 8 9 10

7a Hotels

Vocabulary

Travel: nouns

1 Match the words with the definitions. Then check in a dictionary.

cruise expedition ~~journey~~ safari
tour trek trip voyage

We go on a ? when we ...

travel a long distance. *journey*

1 go somewhere for a short time. ......
2 visit many places by water. ......
3 visit many places by land. ......
4 travel a long distance by sea or in space. ......
5 travel a long and difficult route on foot. ......
6 go to see wild animals. ......
7 travel to a special place to do or find something important. ......

VOCABULARY PAGE 128, 7.2

2 Listen and check. Repeat the words.

Listening

3 Listen to the travel programme. Look at pictures a–d. Which hotels do the presenters talk about?

4 Are the sentences true or false? Listen again and check.

1 People have to wear diving equipment in the undersea lodge.
2 Felicity needed special clothes in her hotel.
3 Visits to a space hotel will definitely be possible in 2010.
4 If you want to go to the space hotel, you'll need seventy million euros.
5 If David had the opportunity, he'd go into space.
6 Felicity is thinking of staying in a hotel this summer.

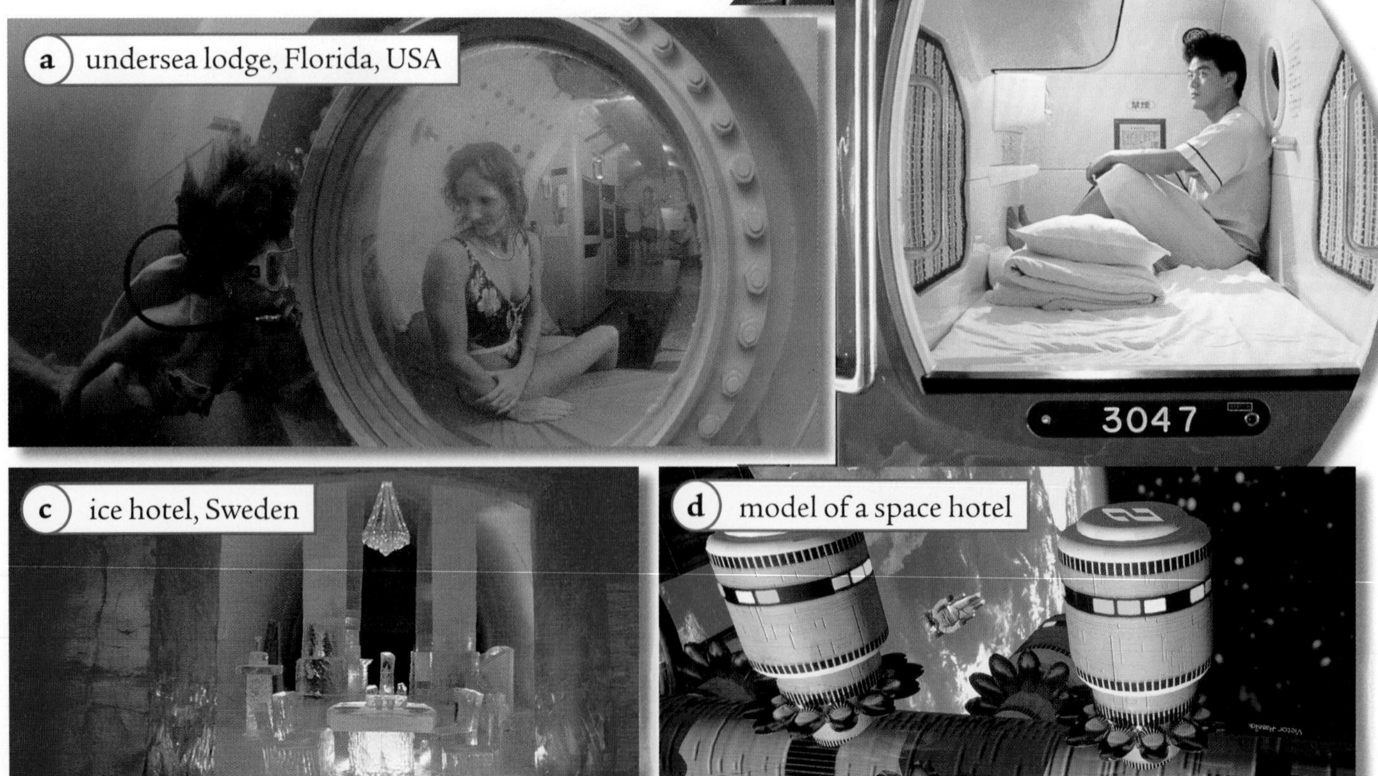

a undersea lodge, Florida, USA

b capsule hotel, Japan

c ice hotel, Sweden

d model of a space hotel

Exploring grammar

Relative clauses

Relative clauses give important information about a noun. We use the relative pronouns *who*, *which* and *that* to form relative clauses.

5 Look at the examples. Then choose the alternative to complete the rules.

I found a hotel **which** is underwater.
I stayed at a hotel **that** was really cold!
There are lots of people **that** want to try it.
They're looking for tourists **who** are rich.

Rules

1 We use the relative pronoun **which** for **people** / **things** / **both**.
2 We use the relative pronoun **who** for **people** / **things** / **both**.
3 We use the relative pronoun **that** for **people** / **things** / **both**.
4 We **use** / **don't use** a subject pronoun in the relative clause.

GRAMMAR PAGE 120

6 Complete the text with *who* and *which*.

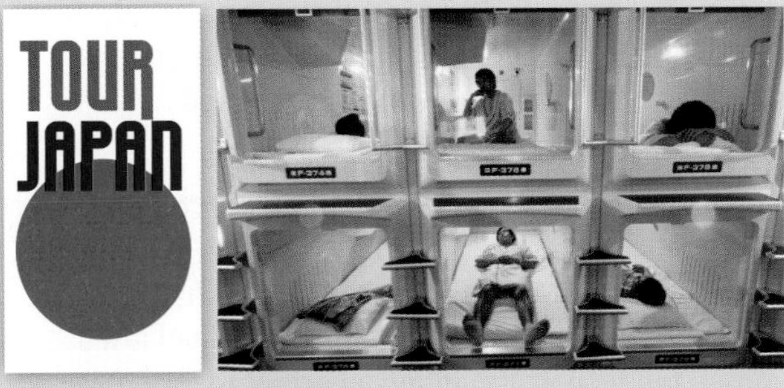

Capsule hotels: the facts

Capsule hotels are cheap hotels in Tokyo *which* don't have rooms.

1 They have small beds ...... are in boxes in the wall.
2 Capsule hotels aren't for tourists ...... want to stay for a long time.
3 Most tourists want all the services ...... normal hotels offer.
4 People ...... stay in capsule hotels usually need a bed for one night.
5 Capsule hotels are often used by local workers ...... have missed their last train home.

7 Join the sentences together. Rewrite them with *who*, *which* or *that*.

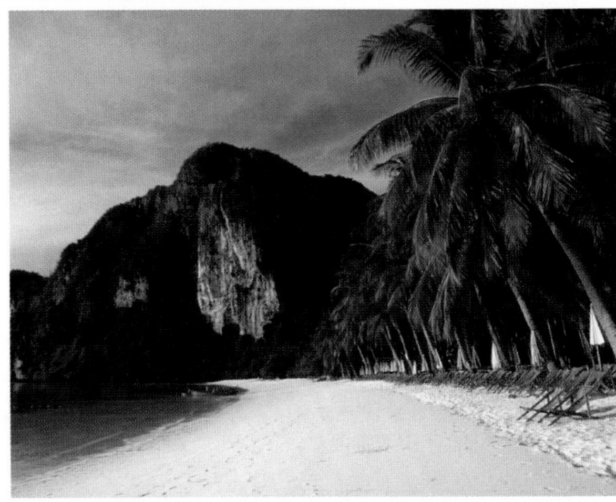

I stayed at a fantastic hotel.
The hotel was really different.

I stayed at a fantastic hotel which was really different.

OR

I stayed at a fantastic hotel that was really different.

1 The owner of the hotel was an old man.
He was very interested in the natural world.
2 The hotel was on a beautiful beach.
The beach had forest all around it.
3 Most of the guests were tourists.
They wanted to see the amazing animals and fish.
4 The hotel had professional divers.
They taught the guests to dive.
5 There were several large boats.
The boats took the guests out to the islands.
6 Some of the boats had special floors.
The floors were made of thick glass.

Finished?

Which of the hotels on pages 72 and 73 would you like to stay at? Why?

I'd like to stay at the capsule hotel because ...

7b Around the world

Reading

1 **Read and listen. How many countries and continents does the text mention?**

2 **Read the article again and match places a–f on the map with the sentences about Dave's journey.**

1 Dave and John started to use the wagon.

2 Dave started to walk with Peter.

3 Dave started to walk with John.

4 Dave met Jenni Samuel.

5 Dave and Peter finished the Asian part of the trip.

6 Dave and John were given a second mule.

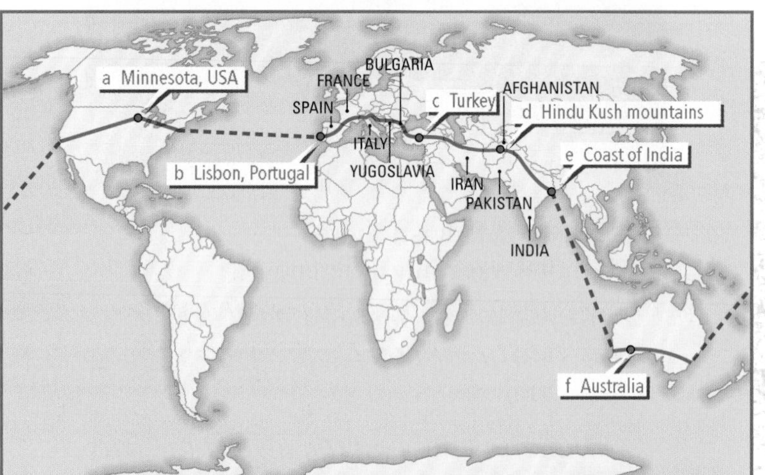

Walking around the world

Dave Kunst is an experienced traveller. In 1974, he became the first person to walk around the world. He started on 20 June 1970 from Minnesota, USA. Four years, three months and sixteen days later, Dave finished his journey in the same place, after travelling 23,120 kilometres across many different countries and continents. On his journey he used twenty-one pairs of shoes and walked more than twenty million steps. His story is both happy and sad.

Dave began his journey with his brother John and a mule. They crossed the USA on foot. Then they sold the mule and flew to Portugal, where they were given a new mule. The journey across Europe was fun. The brothers enjoyed the journey although they had a lot of language problems. In Turkey they bought a wagon to transport enough food and water for their trek across the deserts of Iran and Afghanistan.

In Asia, their journey became harder. Deserts are always dangerous places, and in the Desert of Death, Afghanistan, the temperature reached 53°C. Bandits are another problem in that area, and later tragedy struck. They were attacked near the Hindu Kush mountains while they were walking peacefully. Dave was shot and injured, and his brother, John, was killed. After some time in hospital, Dave returned to the Hindu Kush mountains and started to walk again, this time with another brother, Peter. They started to walk again from where John had died. They finished the trek across Asia in northern India and crossed the Indian Ocean to Australia.

In Australia, Dave lost two companions. After a year of walking with Dave, Peter returned to his job in the USA. Then, a few days later, Dave's Australian mule died. With a wagon but no mule, Dave had a problem. Luckily he met a woman called Jenni Samuel, who offered to pull the wagon behind her car while Dave walked.

One thousand, six hundred kilometres later, Dave and Jenni had fallen in love. However, they still couldn't stay together because Dave had to fly to the USA to complete his journey. When Dave finally finished, he had crossed four continents and thirteen countries. He had lost a brother, but he had also found a partner to love. Dave and Jenni finally got married after he had finished his round-the-world walk.

John Dave Peter

Exploring grammar

Articles: *a / an*, *the* and no article

3 Look at the examples and complete the rules with *a / an* and *the*.

Dave began with his brother and **a mule**.
Then they sold **the mule** and flew to Portugal.
In Europe, they enjoyed **the journey**.
He became **the first person** to walk around **the world**.

Rules

1 We use ...... when we first mention one of something.
2 We use ...... when:
- we mention a specific thing or things again.
- the context tells us which specific things we mean.
- there is only one of them.

GRAMMAR ▶ PAGE 120

4 Circle the correct articles.

Edna went on (an) / **the** interesting journey across Egypt. She started (**1**) **a** / **the** journey in (**2**) **a** / **the** small boat on the River Nile. Edna liked (**3**) **a** / **the** boat because it was slow and quiet, and she had (**4**) **a** / **the** good time. After that, she found (**5**) **an** / **the** old man who sold animals. Edna bought (**6**) **a** / **the** camel from (**7**) **a** / **the** man to ride across the desert. Very soon Edna discovered that she had (**8**) **a** / **the** problem. (**9**) **A** / **The** problem was that she couldn't control (**10**) **a** / **the** camel. It didn't understand English!

5 Complete the text with *a / an*, *the* and a line (—) where no article is necessary.

I love ~~....~~ safaris. I'd like (**1**) ...... holiday in Africa.

I went on (**2**) ...... trip to Warsaw and (**3**) ...... trip to Paris last year. (**4**) ...... trip to Warsaw was great.

I think (**5**) ...... cruises are great, but they're expensive.

I love New York. I've been up (**6**) ..... Statue of Liberty and (**7**) ...... view is amazing.

Articles and geographic names

6 Find examples in the text on page 74 and complete the rules with *the* or no article.

Rules

1 We use ...... with most **countries**.
2 We use ...... with countries that have **States**, **Kingdom** or **Republic** in their names.
3 We use ...... with **oceans**, **seas** and **rivers**.

7 Write *the* where it is necessary. Put a line (—) where no article is necessary.

A trip to *the* USA is a great way to practise your English, but for people from ~~.....~~ Europe, (**1**) ...... UK is cheaper because you don't have to cross (**2**) ...... Atlantic Ocean. In (**3**) ...... UK you can visit (**4**) ...... England, (**5**) ...... Scotland and (**6**) ...... Wales. If you prefer somewhere warmer, (**7**) ...... Malta and (**8**) ...... Cyprus have lots of English speakers, and they are in (**9**) ..... Mediterranean Sea – very sunny!

Pronunciation

***the*: /ðɪ/ or /ðə/ ?**

8 Listen to the different pronunciation of *the*. Decide which words are pronounced /ðɪ/ and which /ðə/. What is the rule? Listen and check.

the Alps the Amazon the Equator
the Himalayas the Indian Ocean
the Mediterranean Sea the Sahara

/ðɪ/	/ðə/
the Atlantic	the Pacific

Speaking

9 Tell your partner what you know about the places in exercise 8. Which of these would you like to visit? Why / Why not?

Finished?

Write about your ideas from exercise 9.

7c Travelling companions

Reading

1 Complete the questionnaire.

Speaking

2 Work in pairs. Compare your answers. How many of your answers are the same? Check the key.

Listening

3 Listen to the dialogue. Why is Paula angry?

4 Listen again and choose the correct alternative.

1 Jim wants to go to the *beach* / *museum*.
2 He wants to *drive* / *ride* there.
3 Paula arrives at the café at *11.00* / *12.00*.
4 *Paula* / *Sylvie* wants to go to the beach.
5 Jim is a *waiter* / *customer* at the café.

The perfect travelling companion!

Compare your answers with a friend. How much have you got in common?

1 Would you prefer a holiday abroad or in your own country?
2 Do you prefer activity holidays, lazy holidays, or a mix?
3 Does your perfect travelling companion have to be extrovert?
4 Do you snore or talk in your sleep?
5 Do you prefer sightseeing or shopping?
6 Have you ever made friends on holiday?
7 Would you like to go on holiday without your parents?
8 Have you ever thought about travelling around the world?
9 Do you think that camping is fun or a nightmare?
10 Do you like being in the country, or do you prefer city life?
11 Would you like to go on holiday in a big group?
12 Do you think that you could survive if you were lost in a forest or a jungle?
13 Would you like to try bungee jumping?
14 Do you mind eating food from other countries?
15 If you had the opportunity, which would you buy: a plane or a yacht?

Key How many of your answers are the same?

0–4 answers the same

Oh, dear. You aren't ideal travelling companions. In fact, if you went on holiday with this person, it would be a total disaster. It would be better if you went to different continents for your holidays!

5–10 answers the same

You and your partner have got some things in common, and you'd probably have a good time if you travelled together. Sometimes it's good to be with people who are different from you. However, there is a chance that your partner would get on your nerves.

11–15 answers the same

Congratulations! You've found the perfect travelling companion. You've got a lot of things in common, and if you went on holiday together you'd have a really great time. Where are you going to go?

Writing

An informal letter

We often use a conversational style in an informal letter. We use special expressions to introduce ideas or to change the topic.

5 Read the letter. Copy and translate the expressions which are in blue

Dear Jim,

Hi! Do you remember me from the summer? You were working in a café and I used to come in every day. I said that I'd write to you, so that's what I'm doing.

Where shall I start? I haven't got much news. I've been out a few times, but not with my friend Paula. She hasn't spoken to me since the holidays! My friends and I have found a new club. We'll have to go there if you visit! What else? Oh, yes, I've painted my room purple. It looks good now.

What about you? Have you got a girlfriend? Do you still watch the football every Saturday? I've still got the West Ham shirt that you gave me.

Well, Jim, I must go. I have to do my homework. It would be great to hear from you.

I'm going to go to Cornwall on holiday again next year, so I might see you! I hope so.

Please write and tell me your news. Bye for now.

Love,

6 Match expressions 1–4 with uses a–d.

We use this expression:

1	Where shall I start?	**3**	What about you?
2	What else?	**4**	Well, I must go.

a when we ask a person about their news.

b when we are thinking of what to write at the beginning of a letter.

c when we are going to finish the letter.

d when we are trying to think of more news.

7 Imagine that you met a person on holiday. Write a letter. Use the expressions in exercise 6. Think about these things:

- Where did you both meet?
- What were you both doing?
- What have you done since your holiday?
- What do you want to ask the person?
- What are your plans for the summer?
- What do you have to do now?

Study skills

Checking your written work

You should always check these things in your written work:

- grammar
- spelling
- punctuation
- vocabulary

8 Read Magda's letter. Match problems 1–4 with her teacher's comments a–d.

Dear Andy,

Do you remember me from your holiday last summer? We (1) meet on the beach. We (2) didnt swim because of the (3) terible weather.

Do you still (4) play windsurfing?

---

a Check your spelling. Use a dictionary.
b Check your grammar, Magda. Use the correct tense.
c This is the wrong word here. What should it be?
d Check your punctuation – remember contractions.

9 Check your partner's letter from exercise 7.

Finished?

Describe your ideal travelling companion.

My ideal travelling companion would prefer holidays abroad.

Progress Check 7

Geographical features

1 Complete the sentences. Use the words in the box.

island
ocean
~~continents~~
forest
equator
lake
poles

There are six *continents* on Earth.

1 Land with water all around it is an ....
2 A large area of trees is a ....
3 Water with land all around it is a ....
4 The ...... goes around the middle of the Earth.
5 The ...... are at the most northerly and southerly points of the Earth.
6 The Atlantic is an ....

Travel: nouns

2 Put the letters in the correct order.

prit *trip*

1 terk	3 ruto	5 icesur
2 yogeva	4 jeyruno	6 afairs

Relative clauses

3 Circle the correct words.

There's a hotel in Boston, USA **who** / **which** doesn't have any door keys. The hotel uses technology (**1**) **who** / **that** can recognize guests' eyes. People (**2**) **who** / **which** wear glasses can also use the technology. Nine Zero Hotel is the only hotel (**3**) **who** / **which** keeps photographs of its guests' eyes. Guests (**4**) **which** / **that** come to Nine Zero again don't have to check in. People (**5**) **who** / **which** have used the new technology think it's great.

Articles

4 Complete the text with *a*, *an*, *the* and — (no article).

All — young people love (**1**) ...... adventures, but Ffyona Campbell thought of (**2**) ...... amazing idea. She decided to be (**3**) ...... first woman to walk around (**4**) ...... world. At 18 years old, she started her incredible journey of 31,536 km.

When she finally finished, people were waiting to celebrate her triumph. But later Ffyona told the truth about (**5**) ...... trek. She explained that she had travelled 1,609 kilometres in (**6**) ...... vehicle with her boyfriend. One year later, Ffyona returned to (**7**) ...... USA and walked those 1,609 km again. She said, 'It's difficult to live with a lie!'

5 Read the quiz. Choose the correct answers from the box. Add *the* where necessary.

Atlantic Czech Republic Italy Nile
English Channel Greece Thames USA

QUIZ

1 Where were the Olympics in 2004?
....
2 Which country has Prague as its capital?
....
3 Which ocean lies between Africa and South America?
....
4 What is the famous river in Egypt?
....
5 Which country has Rome as its capital?
....
6 Where is Texas?
....
7 Which sea is between France and Britain?
....
8 Which river runs through London?
....

On screen

Have a look!

Find the pages where you:

- **write questions for a game show.**
- **talk about television.**
- **listen to a programme about the history of computer games.**

Vocabulary

TV programmes

1 Match pictures 1–8 with the programmes in the box. Which programmes are not illustrated? Listen and check.

the news · the weather · drama series · documentary · soap opera · ~~chat show~~ · game show · comedy · cartoon · sports programme · music programme

1 chat show

2 Listen and identify the programmes.

1 chat show

VOCABULARY PAGE 128, 8.1

Speaking

3 In pairs, give your opinions about your likes and dislikes.

A: For me, documentaries are the best.

B: Really? I think they're boring.

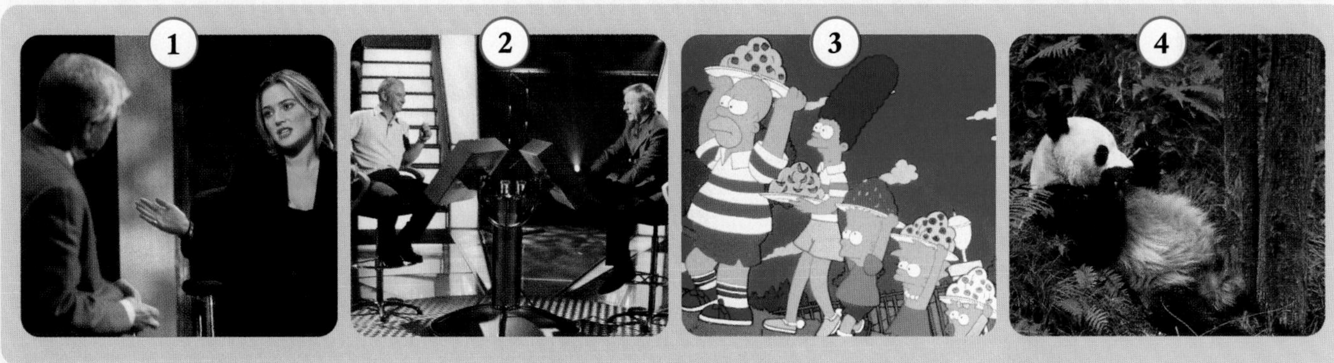

8a Prize money

Reading

1 Quickly find the numbers in the text. Then match them with the information a–d.

125,000 30 14 240,000

a The number of people who phone a game show.

b The age of a famous contestant.

c The money people can win on game shows.

d The number of weeks one person was on a show.

2 Read the text again. Are these sentences true or false?

1 The first game shows were seen in the 1960s.

2 The TV company gave the answers to Van Doren.

3 The *Twenty-one* fraud wasn't discovered.

4 Van Doren became successful after he left the show.

5 Each new contestant is chosen by phone.

6 Most candidates for shows aren't accepted.

PRIZE MONEY

And is that your final answer? You've just won £125,000!

Who wants to be a millionaire?

Will the contestant be lucky and win a big prize in *Who wants to be a millionaire?* For millions of viewers every week, this is a very exciting moment. The programme is addictive and is watched every week by millions of viewers. They feel the tension the contestant feels as they try to answer the questions. Game shows are not a new phenomenon. They were first shown on American TV in the 1950s and they were an instant success. If contestants answered questions correctly, they were invited to appear on the next show. Some contestants even became famous. One of them, a 30-year old university professor called Charles Van Doren, appeared for 14 weeks on a quiz show called *Twenty-one*.

But there was a secret behind Van Doren's success. Because he was very popular with the viewers, the TV company wanted him to continue winning. Therefore, every week, Van Doren received an envelope from the TV company containing the questions and answers for the next show. This fraud wasn't discovered until another contestant complained, and eventually Van Doren confessed. The show was stopped and the professor's career was ruined.

Twenty-one

These days scandals are not common. Questions are written by teams of experts, and they are a secret until the evening of the show. Contestants are selected after they have phoned the TV station and answered questions quickly and correctly. There are telephone competitions before the final selection is made for *Who wants to be a millionaire?* In the USA, 240,000 calls are received for each show, but very few people are selected. So, if you're interested, remember: you need to be fast, intelligent and very, very lucky.

Exploring grammar

The passive (present and past simple): affirmative and negative

3 Look at the sentences in exercise 2. Complete the table with *is, aren't, wasn't* and *were*.

Present simple passive		
Each contestant	(1) ...... isn't	chosen by phone.
Most candidates	are (2)	accepted.
Past simple passive		
The fraud	was (3)	discovered.
The first shows	(4) ...... weren't	seen in the 1960s.
by		
The show is watched **by** millions of viewers.		

GRAMMAR PAGES 120–121
IRREGULAR VERBS INSIDE FRONT COVER

4 Write about Music Quiz using points 1–7. Use the correct present or past form of the passive.

Music Quiz

We started Music Quiz in June.
Music Quiz was started last June.

1 We transmit two programmes every week.
2 Two young people present the show.
3 Famous radio presenters write the questions.
4 A 14-year-old boy won £100,000.
5 About 2 million people usually watch Music Quiz.
6 Almost 3 million viewers saw it last week.
7 Audiences voted Music Quiz the best new programme.

The passive (present and past simple): questions

5 Study the table. Then translate sentences 1–4.

Present simple passive
(1) How **are** contestants **chosen**?
(2) **Are** most candidates **accepted**?
Past simple passive
(3) When **were** the first game shows **seen**?
(4) How **was** the *Twenty-one* fraud **discovered**?

6 Complete the questions. Use the present or past form of the passive. Then answer the questions.

GAME SHOW QUESTIONS

Entertainment
1 Which Disney films about toys *were created* using computer images? *Toy Story 1 and Toy Story 2*

Sport
2 Which famous league ...... (win) six times by the Chicago Bulls in the 1990s?

Technology
3 In which century ...... computers ...... (invent)?

Science and nature
4 In which hemisphere ...... penguins normally ...... (find)?

History
5 In which century ...... the recipe for chocolate ...... (take) to Europe?

Art and architecture
6 Where ...... the Eiffel tower ...... (build)?

Music
7 What type of music ...... (compose) by Mozart (1756–1791)?

General knowledge
8 Which languages ...... (speak) in Canada?

Finished?

Write game show questions.
When was TV invented?

8b Computer games

Vocabulary

Human achievement: verbs and nouns

1 Complete the table. Then listen and check.

Verb	Noun (person)	Noun (things)
entertain	entertainer	*entertainment*
compete	(1)	(2) ......
(3)	(4)	invention
compose	(5)	composition
(6)	explorer	(7) ......

VOCABULARY PAGE 128, 8.2

Reading

2 Read the article. Then complete the text with words from the table in exercise 1.

MAKING GAMES RADIO 1 20:00

The companies that dominate the computer games market make a lot of money. They also spend a lot. The advertising to launch a game is expensive, and companies spend millions as they *compete* to design the best game with the best graphics.

Games companies use expert programmers and other specialists for every part of the game's design and development. For example, for a new game, they have the scenes drawn by artists and have the music written specially by professional (1) ....

Another recent change has come from the cinema. *The Matrix* is not only a film; it has become a popular computer game too. As you read this, other film companies are having games made from their new films. You will see the adverts for the games when you watch the films at the cinema.

Computer games are great (2) .... for millions of people. There are multi-game consoles that allow you to (3) ...... the universe or be a (4) ...... in a golf championship. But when and how did computer games start? What was the first game and who was its (5) ......? Who knows...?

Listening

3 Listen to the history of computer games and order inventions a–f.

1 d

a consoles with more than one game
b games with more than one level
c consoles with internet connections
d the first video game
e the Gameboy
f games with CD ROMs

4 Listen again and answer the questions.

1 Why was Pong an important game?
2 What are Atari and Nintendo?
3 Which character became Mario?
4 When did people start to use CD ROMs?
5 Who was worried about pupils in Japanese schools?
6 Why do games have age certificates in some countries?

Exploring grammar

Causative *have* (*have something done*)

We use causative *have* when people don't do the action themselves but somebody does it for them.

5 Complete the sentences from the article. Then choose the correct rule.

1 Computer companies ...... the scenes ...... by artists.
2 They ...... music ...... for a new game
3 Film companies ...... games ...... from their films.

Rule

We form causative **have** with a tense of **have** + noun + **present** / **past** participle.

GRAMMAR PAGE 121
IRREGULAR VERBS INSIDE FRONT COVER

6 Complete the text with causative *have*.

Lana is a manager in a computer games company. She doesn't design any games, she *has* them *designed* by teams of experts. Then her assistants (**1**) ...... the CDs ...... (copy) in China.

Lana is always looking for ways to make the games better, so she (**2**) ...... new games ...... (test) by groups of young people. They play the games and make suggestions. Lana (**3**) ...... the suggestions ...... (send) to her computer programmers. Then they try to use the ideas in the games. Lana likes to choose the music for the games, and she often (**4**) ...... new music ...... (compose). Her designers sometimes make games from popular films, and they (**5**) ...... videos ...... (make) of the actors. The programmers use images from the videos.

At the moment, her team are working on a new game about the year 2199. It's called *Space Wars*.

7 What is happening? Write the sentences with causative *have*.

He / have / his shoes / polish.
He's having his shoes polished.

1 She / have / her hair / cut.
2 She / have / her nails / paint.
3 He / have / his face / make up.
4 He / have / a costume / make.
5 They / have / some photos / take.

Pronunciation

Word stress: number of syllables

8 Listen and repeat. How many syllables has each word got? Write *2*, *3* or *4*. Then mark the stress.

competitor – 4 syllables

1 competition
2 inventor
3 invention
4 compose
5 entertain
6 entertainer

Finished?

Describe a computer game that you know. Explain why you like the game.

SportMEGA is a football game. I like it because ...

8c Television

Listening

1 Guess the correct answers. Then listen and check.

1 When was television invented?
a 1904 b 1914 c 1924 d 1934

2 How many televisions were there before 1937?
a 1,500 b 15,000 c 150,000 d 1,500,000

3 When were the first colour programmes?
a 1931 b 1951 c 1971 d 1981

4 How many free channels are there in Britain?
a 3 b 5 c 7 d 9

5 How many countries watch MTV?
a 19 b 39 c 59 d 79

2 Listen again and answer the questions.

1 Where was John Logie Baird from?

2 How many people watch television in the world?

3 Which programmes have the most viewers?

4 In Britain, how many teenagers have got a TV in their bedroom?

5 Do British teenagers like American drama series?

6 Which channel do teenagers prefer?

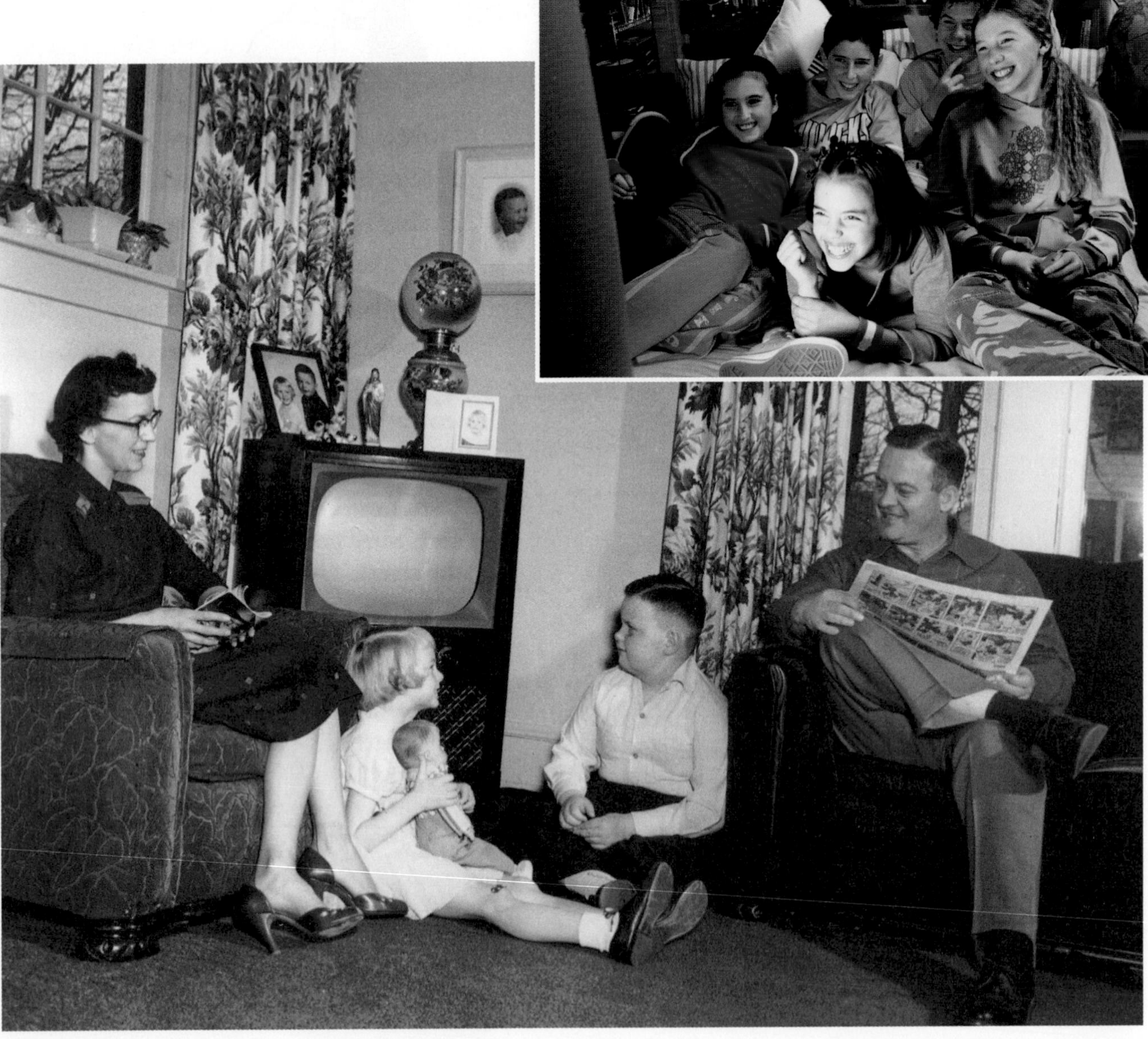

Speaking

3 Work in pairs. Think of good things and bad things about TV.

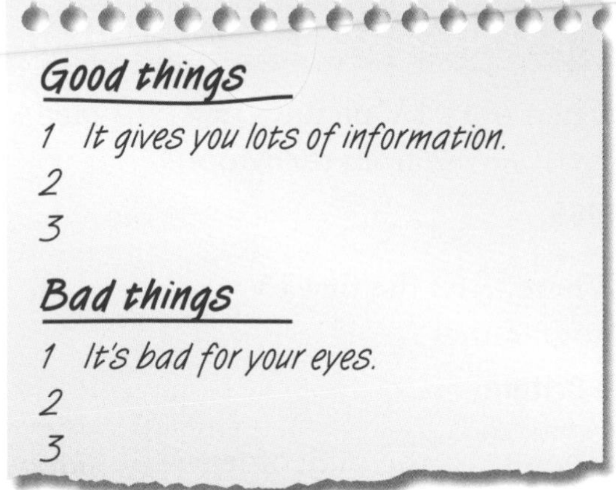

Good things
1 It gives you lots of information.
2
3
Bad things
1 It's bad for your eyes.
2
3

4 Compare your opinions with other people in the class.

A: I think people don't talk when they watch TV.

B: I disagree.

Reading

5 Read the text quickly. What is it?

a a letter
b a poem
c an essay
d an email

Are computer games anti-social and unnecessary? Computer games are becoming more popular, especially with young people. People often can't decide, however, if computer games are good or bad.

On the one hand, computer games are great when you want to relax. They also teach you to think faster, and some games can teach you new skills. For example, there are training programmes that teach you to drive trains or fly aeroplanes. So computer games are good in many respects.

On the other hand, computer games are often very violent. Some psychologists think that the violence in games makes the players more aggressive and unfriendly. Also, when people spend a lot of time playing computer games, they don't go out and they don't talk to their friends or family.

In conclusion, computer games are useful entertainment, but they can become anti-social if people play them too much.

6 Read the text again. Are these sentences true or false?

The writer thinks that:

1 People are not always sure that computer games are good.
2 People can't learn anything from computer games.
3 There might be dangers in playing computer games.
4 Computer games make people friendlier.
5 People shouldn't play any computer games.

Writing

A 'for and against' composition

7 Look at the text again. Match the paragraphs with the information in a–d.

Paragraph 1 ......
Paragraph 2 ......
Paragraph 3 ......
Paragraph 4 ......

a It describes the good points about the topic.
b It brings the good and bad points together and makes a decision.
c It tells the reader what the essay is about.
d It describes the bad points about the topic.

8 Write an essay with the title 'Is television good or bad?'

- Use your ideas from exercise 3.
- Use the expressions in blue from exercise 5.
- Use the plan from exercise 7.

Finished?

Invent a Saturday schedule for your TV station. Include at least six different types of programme.

9.00 science fiction drama series
9.40 cartoons

Progress Check 8

TV programmes

1 Complete the programmes with the missing vowels.

g_m_ sh_w *game show*

1 dr_m_ s_r_ _s
2 s_ _p _p_r_
3 c_rt_ _n
4 c_m_dy
5 _h_ w_ _ th_r

Human achievement: verbs and nouns

2 Complete the sentences. Use the words in the box.

explorer competed invention composer entertainment ~~explore~~

We started to *explore* space in the 1960s.

1 202 countries ...... in the 2004 Olympics.
2 Beethoven was a German ....
3 Radio was Marconi's famous ....
4 The cinema is a great form of ....
5 Captain Cook was a famous ....

3 Complete the sentences. Use the passive.

Present

Many violent games *are banned* (ban).

1 Most consoles .... (make) in Asia.
2 A lot of games ...... (copy) illegally.
3 Consoles from the 1970s ...... (collect) by specialists.

Past

4 More than 13 million Super Mario 3 games ...... (sell) before 2000.
5 The first Tomb Raider game ...... (produce) in 1996.

The passive (present and past simple): questions

4 Complete the questions. Use the correct form of the passive.

TV AND VIDEO QUIZ

1 When *were* TV pictures first *transmitted* from the Moon? **1969.**	*transmit*
2 Where ...... the first TV programmes ......? **In Britain.**	*see*
3 When ...... the camcorder ...... ? **1981.**	*invent*
4 What ...... DVDs ...... from? **Plastic.**	*make*
5 Which TV station ...... in the most countries? **CNN International News.**	*watch*

Causative *have*

5 Write the sentences. Use causative *have*.

Sparkle is a pop star.

hair / do *She has her hair done.*

1 nails / paint
2 clothes / buy
3 meals / cook
4 house / clean
5 letters and emails / answer

All she has to do is be brilliant on stage!

The World of English 4

Round-up 4 (page 88)

Revision: Relative clauses, articles, the passive, causative *have* (*have something done*)

Function: Asking for and giving advice

1 Who needs some advice about Karen?

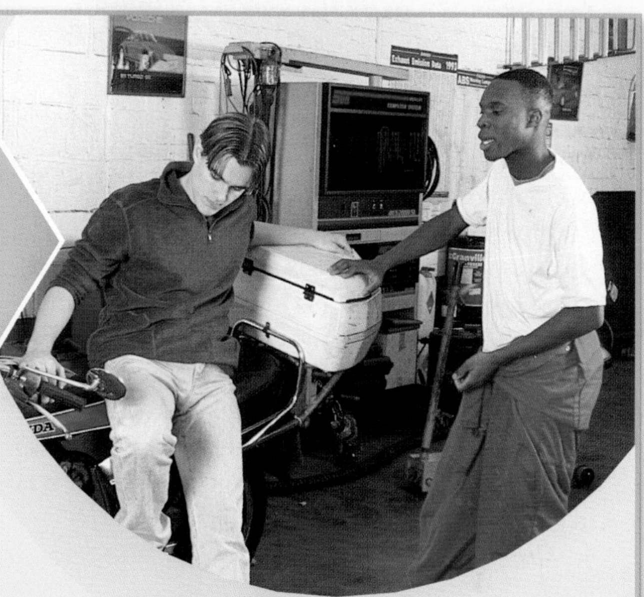

Culture file (page 90)

Topic: Teenage magazines

Vocabulary: Magazine sections

2 How many magazines are published in Britain?

The Story of Pop (page 92)

Artist: Ricky Martin

Type of music: Latin

Song: Livin' la vida loca

3 When did Ricky begin his solo career?

Round-up 4

Relative clauses

1 Decide if the relative pronoun is correct. Put a tick ☑ if it's right, and a cross ☒ if it's wrong. Then write the correct pronoun.

Last year, I had a holiday *that* ☑ was very different. Most people (**1**) *which* ☐ go on holiday want to relax but I went on holiday with people (**2**) *who* ☐ wanted to work! We were in Jordan in the famous city of Petra helping to repair the walls of some of the houses (**3**) *who* ☐ were built in the rock. There were lots of students (**4**) *that* ☐ were studying history like me. We stayed in a hotel (**5**) *which* ☐ was in the middle of Amman, the capital city of Jordan. The people from Jordan (**6**) *which* ☐ were working with us wore traditional clothes, and at times I felt I was living in the past. It was a great experience for a history student!

Articles

2 Complete the text. Use *a, the* or no article

I had always wanted to go on *a* trip around Europe, and so I asked (**1**) .... friend, Lisa, to come with me. We left at 9 a.m. on July 2nd from Waterloo station in London and we took (**2**) .... train to Paris, (**3**) .... French capital. We arrived in Paris early in the afternoon and started looking for (**4**) .... hotel. It was difficult and we didn't get one until 9 p.m.! (**5**) .... hotel was very old and dirty, but we had a place to sleep. We left to go and have something to eat in (**6**) .... café. While we were eating we didn't see (**7**) .... young man sitting at the table next to us. When he got up to leave (**8**) .... café, he quickly took Lisa's bag. We had all our money and our passports in (**9**) .... bag! After three hours at the police station, we had another surprise. Someone had taken all our bags from our hotel room!

The passive

3 Complete the text. Use the words in brackets in the passive tense.

The World Wide Web *was invented* (invent) by Tim Berners-Lee in 1980. Tim Berners-Lee wanted to go from one page of his computer notes to another by clicking on a word. First, a special computer language (**1**) .... (invent). Then it (**2**) .... (give) a name – HTML (HyperText Mark-up Language). Today, Berners-Lee's invention (**3**) .... (use) by Microsoft and Netscape to make internet programmes. Web pages (**4**) .... (design) in the HTML. Berners-Lee now works at the Masachussets Institute of Technology in the USA and all new internet technology (**5**) .... (check) by him. A lot of money (**6**) .... (make) from the internet by some people, but Berners-Lee is more interested in making sure his invention can be used by everyone all over the world.

The causative *have* (*have something done*)

4 Choose the correct form of *have* and write the past participle of the verb in brackets.

Famous film stars live in a different world. They *has* / *(have)* everything (**1**) .... (do) for them and when they travel they stay at the best hotels. Some of them also ask for unusual services. One famous actress (**2**) *has* / *have* all her hotel bedrooms (**3**) .... (paint) in her favourite shade of pink before she arrives. Others (**4**) *has* / *have* their food (**5**) .... (cook) in strange ways by the hotel chefs and some even (**6**) *has* / *have* food from home (**7**) .... (send) them, so they don't have to eat the local meals. Although film stars are strange, so are rock stars. One famous, old British rock star (**8**) *has* / *have* new chairs and tables (**9**) .... (put) in his hotel rooms so he can break them!

Listening

Asking for and giving advice

1 Phil asks Andy for advice on Kim. Listen to the conversation and put the sentences in the order you hear them.

- **a** What would you do? ....
- **b** What shall I do? ....
- **c** Good thinking! Now you're talking! ....
- **d** For a start, you should buy two tickets for the Dido concert on Saturday. ....
- **e** Brilliant! You're a genius! ....
- **f** You should write ... .
- **g** If I were you, I'd send her some flowers. ....
- **h** To be honest, I'm really fed up. ...1...
- **i** I know that, thank you very much! I need ideas. ....
- **j** That's just not my style, and I think I'll need something better than flowers. ....

2 Listen and complete Phil's letter to Kim.

Dear Kim,
I'm (**1**) .... I (**2**) .... your (**3**) ....
Here are two (**4**) .... for the Dido
(**5**) .... Can I (**6**) .... with you?
Love Phil. XXXXX

Useful expressions

3 These expressions were in the story. What do they mean?

1 I'm really fed up.	**3** Now you're talking!
2 That's not my style.	**4** You're a genius!

4 Imagine that a friend needs advice. Think of advice for the people in pictures 1–4.

1 Change your hairstyle.

1 'change my image'

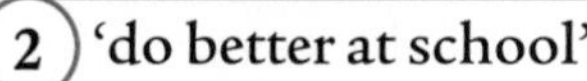

2 'do better at school'

3 'impress a girl'

4 'buy a present for my boyfriend'

Dialogue

Asking for and giving advice

5 In groups of three, discuss your ideas from exercise 4. Use the dialogue below as a model. Substitute the blue words to form your own dialogues.

A: Clare, Kate won't go out with me. What shall I do?

B: Well, if I were you, I'd send her some flowers.

A: No way! That's not my style. What would you do, Mick?

C: Well, for a start, you should buy her a couple of tickets to the concert on Saturday.

A: Right. That's not such a bad idea!

Culture File 4

Magazines

1 Work in pairs. Discuss the questions.

1 What kind of magazines are you interested in?
2 Do you buy any magazines or comics?
3 Would you buy any of the magazines in the picture?

2 Read the facts and the magazine extracts. Are the sentences true or false?

1 Teenzines are a type of internet magazine.
2 Meg advises readers to stay in contact with ex-boyfriends.
3 Eminem's songs are always personal.
4 It is possible to use special 'cheat' codes in the 'Grind Session' game.
5 Juan Sebastian Veron played for Lazio and then played for Boca Juniors.

Vocabulary

Sections in magazines

3 Look at the list of magazine sections. Which sections do extracts a–d come from?

Song lyrics	Competitions
Problem page	Match reports
Game reviews	CD reviews
Player profiles	Tips for games
Questionnaires	Interviews
	News

4 Which sections in exercise 3 would be in your ideal magazine?

Teenage magazines

The facts

- In Britain alone there are 2,794 different magazines. Some of the most popular magazines are for teenagers.
- Teenage girls prefer fashion and lifestyle magazines. Boys prefer magazines about sport and computer games.
- Internet magazines are becoming popular – they are often called teenzines or e-zines.

c Meg's reply

When a boy has split up with you, the worst thing that you can do is phone him. Believe me, it's best to forget him.

a

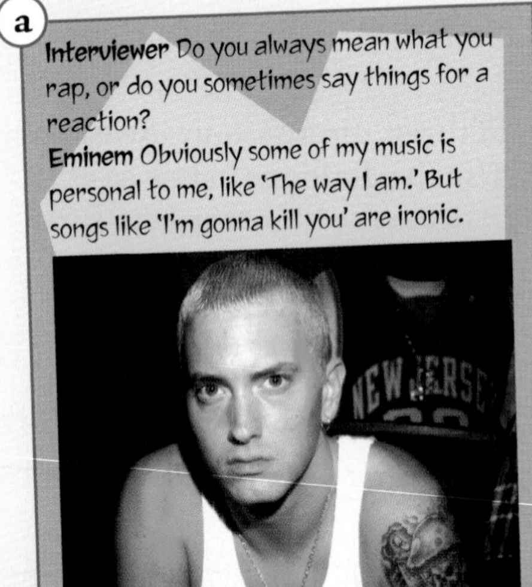

Interviewer Do you always mean what you rap, or do you sometimes say things for a reaction?
Eminem Obviously some of my music is personal to me, like 'The way I am.' But songs like 'I'm gonna kill you' are ironic.

b

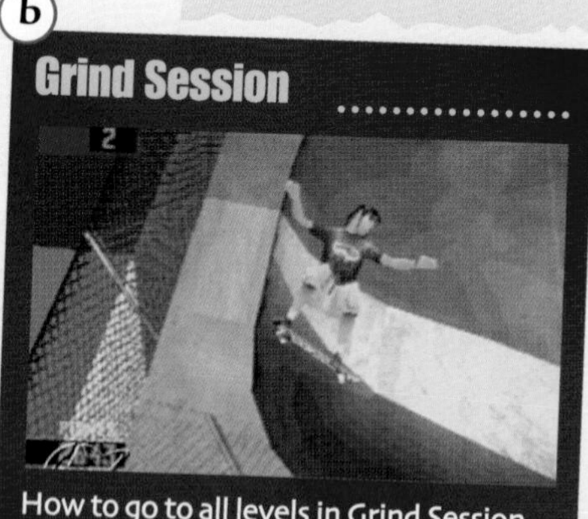

Grind Session

How to go to all levels in Grind Session. Pause the game and use this code: < > ^ ¥. Start the game again and go to the main menu. You can now go to all levels of the game, including the super secret 'Dream House' level.

d

Name: Juan Sebastian Veron
Date of birth: 09/03/75
Height: 1m 86
Nickname: Brujita (little witch)
Position: midfield
First club: Boca Juniors
Other clubs: Manchester United, Chelsea, Inter Milan.
Last transfer fee: £15 million

5 **Listen to the radio programme. When were these teen magazines first published?**

YM ....

Seventeen ....

Tiger Beat ....

6 **Listen again and answer the questions.**

1 Who buys most teen magazines, boys or girls?

2 When did teen magazines become very popular?

3 How many times did YM change its name?

Did you know?

- 33 million Americans are between 12–19 years old; 80% of them read magazines.
- There are around 10,000 magazine titles in the USA.
- 86% of magazines are received in the post, not bought in a shop.
- Newspapers in the USA are produced for local market, e.g. *The New York Times*, but magazines are for the national market.

7 **Tick the subjects Maria says are in magazines today.**

1 fashion ....

2 make-up ....

3 relationships ....

4 sports ....

5 jobs ....

6 teenage problems ....

7 music ....

8 competitions ....

9 computers ....

10 environment ....

Project

Design your own teen magazine.

- What sections would it have?
- What type of information would you put in it?
- Who would you write about?

Design the cover and the contents page, giving a list of the different stories and features. Use photos or drawings.

The Story of Pop 4

Latin music

1 Read and listen. Then answer the questions.

1. How many styles of Latin music does the text mention?
2. Where does Latin music originate from?
3. Why is Latin music great for dancing to?
4. In which languages does Ricky sing on his records?
5. Is Ricky a big star outside Latin America?

Latin music

Latin music is a general term which describes music with origins in Latin America and Central America. A lot of different musical styles come from these areas, for example, salsa, samba, mambo, tejano and bossa nova. The rhythms of most of these types of music are fun and infectious. Latin music is great for dancing because it has got strong, happy rhythms. For this reason, it has become popular all over the world.

Ricky Martin

Ricky Martin was born in Puerto Rico in 1971. He became a star at the age of 13, singing in a Latin boy band called Menudo.

After leaving the group in 1989, he began a solo career, acting on TV and in the theatre, and making records both in Spanish and in English. His high-energy style combines elements of Latin, rock and jazz music.

Ricky has been part of the recent boom in Latin music and he is now an international superstar.

2 Choose the correct words to complete the song. Then listen and check.

Livin' la vida loca

She's into (**1**) **superstition / competition**
Black cats and voodoo dolls.
I feel a premonition
That girl's gonna make me (**2**) **small / fall.**
She's into new sensations
New kicks and candlelight.
She's got a new (**3**) **addiction / discussion**
For every day and (**4**) **night / week.**

She'll make you take your clothes off
And go dancing (**5**) **in Spain / in the rain.**
She'll make you live the crazy life
Or she'll take away your pain
Like a bullet to your (**6**) **brain / chest.**

(Chorus)
Upside, inside out
She's living la vida loca.
She'll push and pull you down
Living la vida loca.
Her lips are devil red
And her skin's the colour mocha.
She will wear you out.
Living la vida loca.
Living la vida loca.
She's living la vida loca.

She'll make you take your clothes off
And go dancing (**7**) **in Spain / in the rain.**
She'll make you live the crazy life
Or she'll take away your pain
Like a bullet to your
(**8**) **brain / chest.**

(Repeat chorus)

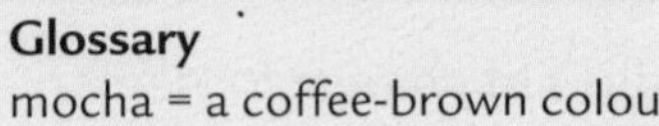

Glossary
mocha = a coffee-brown colour

Messages

Have a look!

Find the pages where you:

- **listen to a radio programme.**
- **write a questionnaire.**
- **read about animals that talk.**

Vocabulary

Reporting verbs

1 Match the verbs in the box with the pictures.

complain	insist	reply	joke
explain	boast	promise	predict

VOCABULARY INSIDE BACK COVER, 9.1

Speaking

2 Think of statements to match the verbs, then say them to your partner. Your partner must guess which verb you are thinking of.

A: I'll buy lunch for you.

B: promise

9a Animal talk

Reading

1 Read the article quickly. Match the animals in the box with the paragraphs.

apes bees dolphins monkeys

Paragraph 1 ...... Paragraph 3 ......
Paragraph 2 ...... Paragraph 4 ......

2 Read the article again and answer the questions.

1 Which insects does the article mention?
2 Which monkeys does the article describe, and how many calls do they make?
3 What type of animals are studied in Julia Bell's experiments?
4 Why did the first scientists have a problem with apes?
5 How good is Kanzi at communicating?
6 Which animals in the article have learned to communicate with humans?

Animals and language

Seventy years ago, Karl von Frisch discovered that bees dance to tell each other where to find food. He insisted that bees could communicate better than birds. He won a Nobel Prize for his studies.

In the animal kingdom, vervet monkeys use 36 different calls to communicate, including alarm calls for different kinds of danger. When they hear different calls they behave differently. When they hear the call that means snake, they stand up and look around, but when they hear the call that means eagle, they jump in the bushes to hide.

According to Julia Bell, a researcher, we shouldn't be surprised that more intelligent animals have better 'language' skills. In a recent interview she said, 'We know that animals communicate. Even insects communicate. Today scientists are teaching different types of animals to communicate with us. They started with apes and they have had some success. My team work with dolphins and we're making good progress in our project. The dolphins are learning. We've taught them to use special symbols, and we can understand each other. Of course we still don't know what they talk about in the wild – I'm not sure we'll ever know everything'.

Research on communication between humans and apes started in the 1930s, when scientists started teaching chimpanzees. They found the apes could follow instructions, for example, when they told them to sit down or not to be noisy they understood. But they soon found that apes couldn't produce many human sounds, so researchers tried other ideas. In the 1960s, a chimpanzee called Washoe and a gorilla called Koko were taught American Sign Language, the system that deaf people use to speak with their hands. Recently, Sue Savage-Rumbaugh has taught chimpanzees to use a keyboard with 400 symbols. Sue believes that her best chimpanzee, Kanzi, uses language like a human child of two and a half years old. Julia Bell says, 'Scientists are becoming more and more interested in animal-human communication. We've known that animals communicate with each other for a long time, but now we can see how 'talking' to animals could help us understand them.'

Exploring grammar

Reported speech

When we report what someone said, the verb tenses change and the pronouns and possessive adjectives usually change.

3 Look at Julia Bell's comments. Then complete the table.

Direct speech	Reported speech
'Even insects communicate.'	Julia Bell said that even insects **communicated**.
'They (1) ……. with apes.'	She said they **had started** with apes.
'They (2) ……. some success.'	She said that they**'d had** some success.
'The dolphins (3) ……. learning'	She said that the dolphins **were** learning.
'We (4) ……. understand each other.'	She said that they **could** understand each other.
Pronouns and possessive adjectives	
'**We** are making progress in **our** project.'	She said that **they** were making progress in **their** project.

GRAMMAR PAGE 121

4 Write these comments in reported speech.

I know that dolphins communicate with each other. (Professor Silvia Black)

She said that she knew that dolphins communicated with each other.

1 The tests with dolphins didn't teach us anything. (Dr Henry Smith)

2 My work has been very useful. (Professor Silvia Black)

3 Humans will never be able to talk to animals. (Dr Henry Smith)

4 In the future, I will learn to understand all animals. (Professor Silvia Black)

5 I can copy bird song, but I can't communicate with birds. (Dr Henry Smith)

Reported instructions

5 Find the reported instructions in the reading text and complete the sentences.

Instructions	Reported instructions
'Sit down.'	They told it (1) …… sit down.
'Don't be noisy.'	They told it (2) …… be noisy.

GRAMMAR PAGE 122

6 What did Gory the gorilla's trainer tell him? Write her instructions in reported speech.

Don't sit on your trainer.

She told him not to sit on his trainer.

1 Give the bananas to me.

2 Don't eat the flowers.

3 Show your picture to me.

4 Don't bite me.

5 Don't climb on the table.

6 Put me down!

Finished?

What are they saying? Write an imaginary conversation between dolphins.

9b Message and meaning

Vocabulary

Communicating information

1 Match the words with the pictures

~~gossip~~ headline lecture signal
slang speech symbol title

1 slang

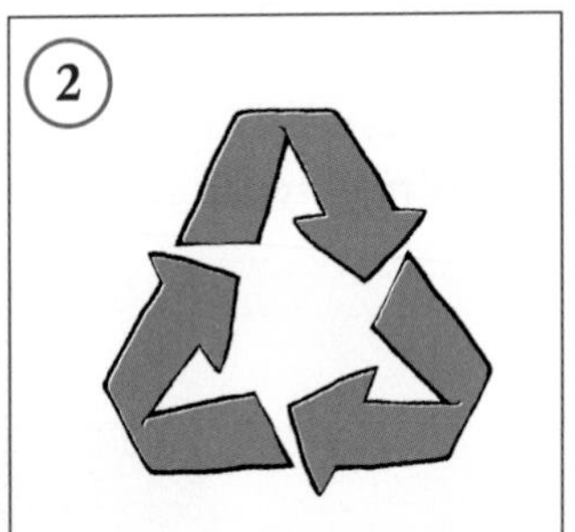

2 Translate the words into your language.

VOCABULARY INSIDE BACK COVER, 9.2

Listening

3 Listen to the radio programme. Match the messages with the meanings.

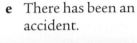

Message:	Meaning:
1 10–50	a very good
2 ...▬ ▬ ▬...	b stairs
3 read and write	c HELP
4 apples and pears	d fight
5 fab	e There has been an accident.

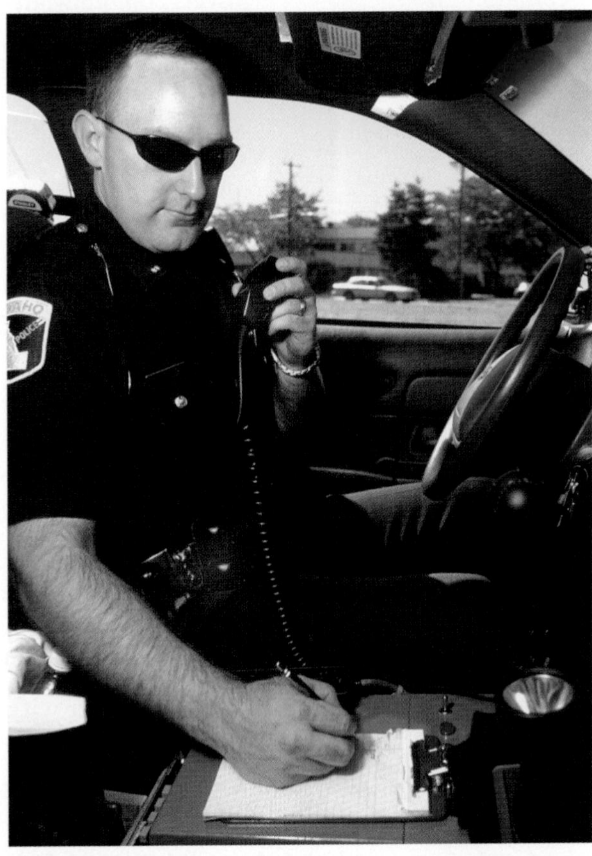

4 Listen to the text again and answer the questions.

1 American police use numbers to communicate. Who else does this?
2 Which is the most famous code?
3 When was Morse code invented?
4 Where did rhyming slang begin?
5 Why does Christy think that Dianne's aunt was a teenager in the 1960s?
6 What is strange about *wicked* as a slang word?

Exploring grammar

Reported speech: questions

5 Look at the underlined parts of the examples. Then complete the rules.

Can Christy use Morse Code?
Matt asked me if you could use Morse Code.
Are all codes secret?
You asked me whether all codes were secret.
Where does rhyming slang come from?
Pete asked us where rhyming slang came from.

Rules

Direct questions have got a question mark.
Reported questions (1) ...... a question mark.
In direct questions there is a verb before the subject.
In reported questions there (2) ...... a verb before the subject.
In questions that have a **Yes** / **No** answer, we use **if** and (3) ...... to report the question.

GRAMMAR ▶ PAGE 122

6 Look at the listeners' e-mails to the programme. What did they want to know? Write their questions in reported speech.

Marta asked them if they could speak much rhyming slang.

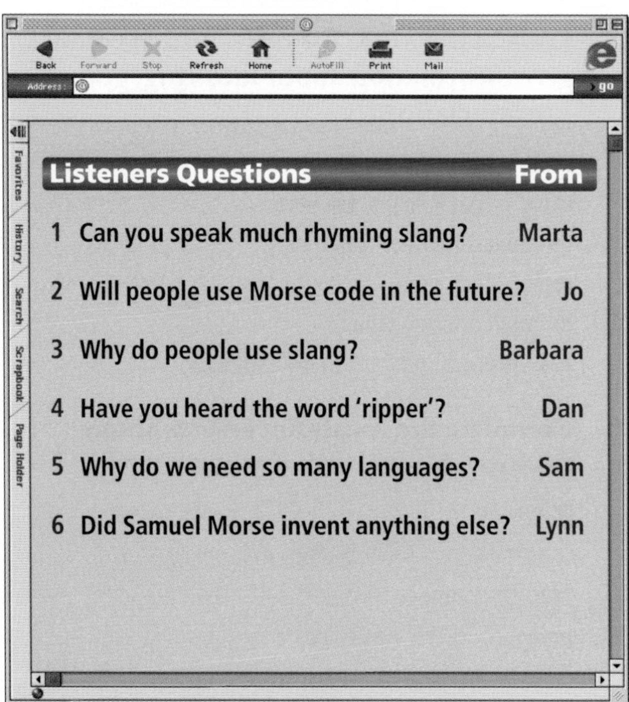

Listeners Questions	From
1 Can you speak much rhyming slang?	Marta
2 Will people use Morse code in the future?	Jo
3 Why do people use slang?	Barbara
4 Have you heard the word 'ripper'?	Dan
5 Why do we need so many languages?	Sam
6 Did Samuel Morse invent anything else?	Lynn

Question tags

7 Look at the examples and choose the correct word to complete the rules.

All codes are secret, **aren't they?**
You wrote about slang, **didn't you?**
Some people can't understand it, **can they?**

Rules

When the first part of the sentence is affirmative, the question tag is **affirmative** / **negative**.
The first part of the sentence and the question tag use the **same** / **different** tenses.

GRAMMAR ▶ PAGE 122

8 Match the question tags with the questions.

hasn't it? are you? ~~wasn't it?~~ didn't you? can they? have you?

The radio programme was good, *wasn't it?*

1 You heard the programme, ...
2 Most people can't use Morse code, ...
3 You aren't going to learn Morse, ...
4 English has always had slang, ...
5 You haven't heard much slang, ...

Pronunciation

Intonation in question tags

9 Listen and repeat. Answer the questions.

1 This is an English lesson, isn't it?
2 You think English is easy, don't you?
3 You aren't from Britain, are you?
4 You've been to Britain, haven't you?

a Does the intonation in the questions go up or down at the end? Draw arrows (↗ or ↘).
b Does it go up when you are sure or unsure?

Finished?

How many words can you make from the letters in 'Message and meaning'? What is the longest word you can make?

9c Get the message

Listening

1 **What are you good at? What kind of information do you understand most easily?**

SATURDAY 18 June

TEEN TALK

In this week's programme, experts describe new ideas on different types of people and different types of intelligence. They look at how we think, learn and communicate. Find out which type you are.

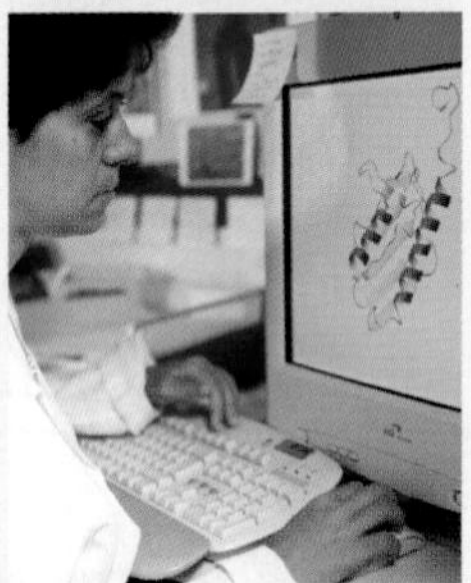

2 **Experts talk about *visual*, *auditory* and *haptic* intelligence. Listen to the interview and match the descriptions with the types of people.**

1 People with visual intelligence
2 People with auditory intelligence
3 People with haptic intelligence

a Hearing information is important to these people.
b Doing things and moving around are important to these people.
c Seeing information is important to these people.

3 **Listen again and choose the correct answer.**

1 How many types of intelligence is Jason Stone interested in?
a 18 types b 8 types c 3 types
2 What type of intelligence has Rachel got?
a visual b auditory c haptic
3 How many people are visual thinkers?
a 70% b 20% c 17%
4 How many people are auditory thinkers?
a 70% b 20% c 17%
5 What type of intelligence has Jason Stone got?
a visual b auditory c haptic

4 **Listen to the end of the interview. Make notes about the advice that Jason gives to the different types of learner.**

visual	auditory	haptic
....	....	....
....	....	....

Study skills

Making vocabulary notes

For new words, it's a good idea to make notes about meaning, pronunciation, grammar and how to put the word into a sentence. You can also use colours to make your notes clearer.

5 **Look at the notes for *reply*. Which colours give information about meaning, grammar, pronunciation?**

reply = answer someone
reply + that + subject + verb
He replied that she was happy.
reply + to + noun
He replied to my email.
past: replied, past participle: replied

6 **Complete the vocabulary notes about promise. Use colours if you want to.**

promise = ...
promise + that + subject + verb
She promised that ...
promise + to + verb
She promised to ...

Reading

7 Read Ewa's report and choose the best title.

1 School project
2 English lessons in our class
3 Questionnaire about learning English
4 Questionnaire about life at school

We did a project at school to find out how people learned English. Two classmates and I wrote a questionnaire to find different information about how people studied. We used different types of question.

Some questions had only *Yes / No* answers. These questions asked whether people had any special ways of remembering new words, and if they used coloured pens when they made notes.

Other questions asked for more information. We asked how much time they spent on homework, and how many different books they used. We also asked what the most difficult thing about learning English was.

The third type of question asked how often people did different things. Four different questions asked how often they read, wrote, spoke or listened to English out of school. The last question asked how often they read their notes. We gave different answers so that they could choose the best one. They could choose from: *very often*, *often*, *sometimes*, *not very often* and *never*.

We gave the questionnaire to some students from other classes, and we got fifty-two replies. We were surprised with the answers because most people practise their English quite a lot. About half of the students often speak English outside the class – some of them record a diary in English! The teacher was very pleased with the results.

6 How often do you read English outside school?
very often ☐ often ☑ sometimes ☐
not very often ☐ never ☐

8 Read Ewa's report again and answer the questions.

1 How many people wrote the questionnaire?
2 Could all the questions be answered with *Yes* or *No*?
3 How many questions did the questionnaire have?
4 How many people answered it?
5 What did the class find out?

Writing

Designing a questionnaire

Questionnaires use different types of question. There are three types we use a lot:

Closed questions ask for *Yes / No* answers:
Do you speak English?

Open questions are *wh* questions that ask for more information:
How long have you studied English?

Graded questions give people different answers that they can choose from:
How good is your English? Put a tick (✓).
Excellent ☐ Good ☐ Not bad ☐ Bad ☐

9 Look at the report in exercise 7 again. How many questions of each type are there?

Closed questions ......

Open questions ......

Graded questions ......

10 Read Ewa's report again carefully and write the class questionnaire.

Speaking

11 Ask and answer the questionnaire with your partner.

Finished?

Make vocabulary notes like the ones in Study skills for other words from this unit.

Progress Check 9

Reporting verbs

1 Choose the correct verb for each sentence.

'Charlie's eating all the fruit!' the chimpanzee **complained** / **predicted**.

1 'We'll never eat it all,' the lion **predicted** / **boasted**.

2 'I can speak English, French and Chimpanzee,' the gorilla **boasted** / **complained**.

3 'She had a surfer for lunch,' Sid Shark **explained** / **promised**.

4 'It won't happen again,' the gorilla **joked** / **promised**.

Communicating information

2 Find and write the words.

lecture

lec head gos sig sl sym spe

ang ech ture bol nal sip line

Reported speech

3 Rewrite the sentences in exercise 1. Use reported speech.

The chimpanzee complained that ...

Reported instructions

4 Report the instructions that the expert gave to people with different types of learners.

Visual learners

'Write notes again in a more organized way.'

He told them to write notes again in a more organized way.

1 'Don't use just black pens.'

Auditory learners

2 'Talk about your notes with friends.'

3 'Record your notes on tape and listen to them.'

Haptic learners

4 'Walk around and repeat important facts.'

5 'Don't sit down for more than half an hour without a break.'

Reported questions

5 Write the questions in reported speech.

Teacher

What type of learner are you?

She asked him what type of learner he was.

1 Are you a visual learner?

2 Have you had any advice about how to study?

Student

3 What did the programme say about visual learners?

4 Will it be easier to study with pictures?

5 Where can I get more information?

Question tags

6 Complete the question tags.

Some people talk to their pets, *don't they?*

1 Animals don't understand everything we say, ...

2 Scientists have taught chimpanzees to communicate, ...

3 Scientists haven't taught them to write, ...

4 It would be useful to understand animals, ...

5 We could find out everything about them, ...

Phenomena

Have a look!

Find the pages where you:

- **read a ghost story.**
- **write about a strange encounter.**
- **listen to a programme about strange powers.**

Vocabulary

Sounds: verbs and nouns

1 Listen and repeat. Then translate the words into verbs and nouns in your language.

1 scream	**4** whistle	**7** shout	**10** hum
2 laugh	**5** whisper	**8** bang	
3 howl	**6** snore	**9** knock	

2 Listen and identify the sounds.

1 whistle

VOCABULARY ▶ INSIDE BACK COVER, 10.1

Speaking

3 Tell the story in pairs. Take turns to describe the pictures.

The man is sleeping and he ...

10a The guardian

Reading

1 Read the ghost story. What is missing from the picture?

The Guardian

I was seventy years old last Thursday. I haven't really celebrated much since my wife Elizabeth died three years ago, but last week I had lunch at my sister's, and later three good friends came to my house for dinner. It was a nice meal. We were talking and laughing, but suddenly I felt sad. I shouldn't have been sad on my birthday, but I'd remembered my wife. She used to love parties. Before a party she used to buy flowers and put them in every room of the house.

Suddenly my thoughts were interrupted. Somebody was knocking at the door. I went to the hall and opened the door. A beautiful young woman was standing there. She may not have been twenty yet, but she was very confident for her age. Her face was pale and her skin was almost transparent. She had some beautiful flowers in her hands and she was smiling. She may have come to the wrong house, I thought.

'Is this Michael's party?' she asked.

'Yes, it is. I'm Michael,' I answered. 'Do I know you?'

'I am Lydia,' she said. 'I am a messenger. I am a guardian.'

Her voice was soft and sweet, but her words were very strange. I thought I might not have heard her correctly.

'A messenger? I don't understand. Who sent you?'

'A friend', she whispered, and she gave me the flowers. 'These are for you. You must have missed your wife terribly since she died. Life can't have been easy, I'm sure. But you should be happy when you think about her. She is always near you, and we protect her. We'll protect you too.'

I don't remember what happened next. I might have looked down at the flowers for a moment. They were roses, my wife's favourite. I started to say thank you to the woman, but when I looked up she wasn't there.

My friend Anne came to the door.

'Who was that?' she asked. 'You should have asked her name. She had the face of an angel.'

'Yes, ...' I said, but it was difficult for me to speak, '... the face ... of an angel.'

2 Read the text again and put sentences a–h in the order they appear in the story.

1 b

a A beautiful woman visited Michael.
b Michael's wife died.
c Michael's wife used to buy flowers.
d The woman gave Michael some flowers.
e A friend spoke to Michael about the woman.
f The woman disappeared.
g Michael had lunch with his sister.
h Michael thought about his wife.

Exploring grammar

Possibility in the past: *may* / *might*, *must* and *can't*

3 Look at the examples and complete the rules.

She **may not have been** twenty yet.
She **may have come** to the wrong house.
I **might not have heard** her correctly.
You **must have missed** her terribly.
Life **can't have been** easy.
I **might have looked** down at the flowers.

Rules

Possibility in the past: affirmative
We use **may** or (1) ...... + **have** + past participle.
Possibility in the past: negative
We use **may** or **might** + (2) ...... + **have** + (3) ....
Certainty in the past: affirmative
We use **must** + (4) ...... + past participle.
Certainty in the past: negative
We use (5) ...... + **have** + past participle.

GRAMMAR ▶ PAGES 122–123

4 Write the sentences about last night with *must* and *can't*.

He / walk / in his sleep.
He must have walked in his sleep.

1 His parents / hear / him.
2 He / make / a lot of noise.
3 He / leave / the bedroom.
4 He / go / outside.
5 He / put / his shoes on.
6 It / be / wet outside.

Speaking

5 Look again at the story in exercise 1. Who was the visitor? Use *might*, *must*, *can't* and the ideas in the box.

a ghost   an angel   Michael's relative
his wife's relative   a friend of his wife

Criticizing past actions: *should have*

When we criticize people's past actions, we use *should* / *shouldn't* + *have* + past participle.

6 Look at the examples and choose the correct words.

I **shouldn't have been** sad on my birthday.
You **should have asked** her name.

Rules

Usually, when we say something **should have happened**, it (1) did / didn't happen.
Usually, when we say something **shouldn't have happened**, it (2) did / didn't happen.

GRAMMAR ▶ PAGE 123

7 Write affirmative and negative sentences with *should have*.

visit / the house
They shouldn't have visited the house.

1 read / the sign
2 stay / outside
3 open / the box
4 run / away

Finished?

Write a story using the sentences in exercise 7.

10b The unexplained

Vocabulary

The explained and unexplained: nouns

1 Match the words in the box with the definitions. Use a dictionary.

experiment ~~belief~~ fact theory trick mystery doubt evidence

something that people believe is true *belief*

1 a possibility that something isn't true ......
2 information we use to decide if something is true or not ......
3 something people can do to find out what is true ......
4 information that we know is definitely true ......
5 something strange that we don't understand ......
6 a possible explanation for phenomena ......
7 a way to make people believe that something is real when it isn't real ......

2 Listen and check. Repeat the words.

VOCABULARY INSIDE BACK COVER, 10.2

3 Complete the texts with the words from exercise 1.

Scientists write a *theory* to explain something. Then they do an **(1)** ...... to find out if their ideas are correct.

Ghosts are a **(2)** ...... and nobody knows if they exist. There's a lot of **(3)** ...... in my mind because I've never seen one.

In the past there was a **(4)** ...... that the world was flat, but the world is round and that's a **(5)** ....

My friend said that she'd seen a UFO, and she showed me a photo as **(6)** .... I knew it was a **(7)** ...... because I could see it was a frisbee!

Listening

4 Listen to the radio programme. Which of these people are in the photos below?

Uri Geller Benedetto Supino
Yvonne Duplessis Erika Zur Stirnberg

5 Listen again and answer the questions.

1 Do the people in the stories really exist?
2 What started to burn while Benedetto Supino was reading?
3 What was Erika Zur Stirnberg doing when she discovered her magnetic powers?
4 What happened to people's watches and clocks while they were watching Uri Geller on TV?
5 How did Yvonne Duplessis stop the children touching the metal?
6 Does the programme explain the phenomena?

Exploring grammar

Obligation, prohibition and necessity

6 Look at the examples and complete the table.

He **didn't need to** touch the objects.
Benedetto **had to** be careful with his powers.
Uri **didn't have to** be in the room with the objects.
She **needed to** be sure there were no tricks.
They **weren't allowed to** touch the metal.

Present	Past
Obligation	
have / has to must	....
Necessity	
have / has to must	....
need to	....
No obligation	
don't / doesn't have to	....
don't / doesn't need to	....
Probitition	
mustn't not be allowed to	....

GRAMMAR PAGE 123

7 Choose the correct words.

Test your special powers

To try this test, you (need to) / don't need to get some cards. They (1) **need to / don't need to** be special, you can use ordinary playing cards. You (2) **need to / don't need to** put the cards face down, so that you can't see what they are. Choose a card but don't pick it up. Try to guess only its colour; you (3) **need to / don't need to** guess exactly what it is. But you (4) **need to / don't need to** concentrate to do the test correctly. When you have decided turn it over and check. Most people (5) **need to / don't need to** practise before they get good scores but with time they do get better.

8 Complete the sentences with the correct form of *need to*. Use the verbs in the box.

ask stand buy sit ~~arrive~~ look

Katy went to see Marvo the Mind Reader. Katy wanted a seat at the front so she *needed to arrive* early.

1 She ...... a ticket because she'd won two tickets in a competition.
2 Marvo chose Katy, so she ...... up.
3 Marvo ...... anything about Katy; he could guess everything.
4 Before Marvo told Katy anything, he ...... into her eyes, and Marvo's eyes were very scary!
5 After Marvo had read her mind, Katy really ...... down.

9 Complete the text with the correct form of *have to* or *not be allowed to*.

Diary — *12th June*

I had to do my homework quickly tonight because I went to see Marvo the Mind Reader. I took my camera, but unfortunately we (1) ...... (take) photos. He invited people on the stage. They (2) .... (accept) but people were interested. He looked into their eyes and guessed lots of facts about them, and they (3) ...... (say) if he was correct or not. They (4) .... (say) more than one word: 'yes' or 'no'. He (5) ...... (meet) anyone before the show, so he didn't know anything about them. But he was correct every time! Amazing!

Finished?

What special power would you like to have and why?

I'd like to know what people are thinking because ...

10c UFO mania!

Listening

1 Listen and order the topics.

a The Romans
b *The War of the Worlds*
c Mass hysteria
d Medieval beliefs

2 Read 1–6. Then listen again and complete the sentences.

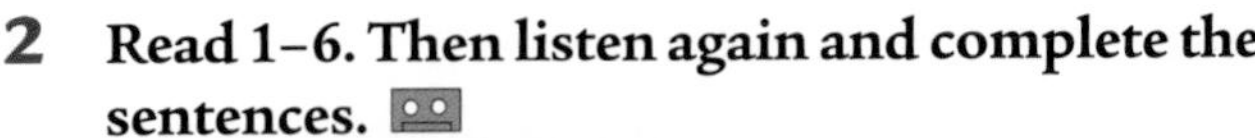

1 When radio listeners heard *War of the Worlds* in 1938, they thought ...
2 Doctor Jarvis thinks that about 95% of UFOs ...
3 She thinks that people want to believe ...
4 Night suns were seen by ...
5 In medieval times, people spoke about ...
6 Miriam didn't believe in UFOs before ...

Reading

3 Read and listen. Find five mistakes in the picture.

A strange encounter

The incident occurred in Randolph Park on 3rd November, 2004. It happened while I was walking with my dog late at night. I was looking peacefully at the stars when, suddenly, I saw this red light. It was moving quickly and quietly towards me. Then it came down really close, and it started to move more slowly. It was very bright, and it was making a strange humming sound. At first, I was fascinated, but then I noticed that there were no other people in the park. I didn't like being alone, and I started to feel scared.

Eventually, after about a minute, the hum became louder, and then it moved east incredibly quickly and disappeared over the trees. I've got no idea what it was, but I don't think that it was from this world. Later, I phoned the police and told them the story. They took my name and address, but they didn't come to interview me. I think that they didn't believe me, but I'm sure that it was a UFO.

UFO MAGAZINE

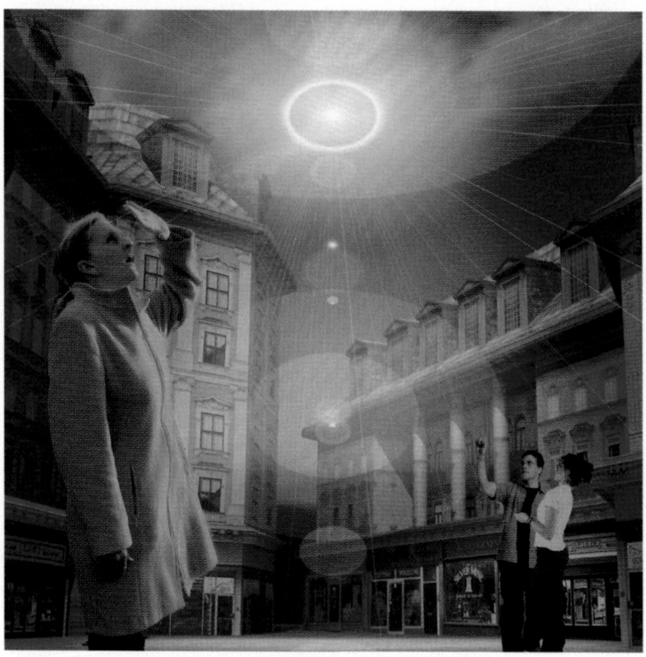

4 Read the story again. Put the newspaper reporter's questions in the correct order.

1 b

- **a** When did the incident occur?
- **b** Where did the incident occur?
- **c** How did the contact end?
- **d** What did you see and hear?
- **e** What were you doing when you saw the object?
- **f** How did you feel at first?

Writing

Using time connectors: *while*, *suddenly*, *at first*, *later* and *eventually*

5 Translate the expressions in bold from Miriam's story into your language.

1. **While** I was walking with my dog ...
2. **Suddenly**, I saw this red light ...
3. **At first**, I was fascinated ...
4. **Eventually**, ... it moved east ...
5. **Later**, I phoned the police ...

6 Write an article about an encounter with a UFO, a ghost or a strange animal.

- Think of new answers for the questions in exercise 4.
- Use the time expressions in the box.

~~while~~ suddenly at first later eventually

Last night I had a strange encounter while I was ...

Finished?

Make a list of unexplained mysteries. Write down any facts, beliefs or theories about them that you know.

UFOs: Some people believe that they come from other planets ...

Progress Check 10

Sounds: verbs and nouns

1 Look at the picture and write sentences. What was happening at ten o'clock last night? Use the words in the box.

howl ~~whistle~~ knock snore shout laugh

1 A man was whistling.

Possibility in the past: *may / might, must* and *can't*

2 Choose the correct word.

In recent years, many sheep around Bodmin in Britain have died mysteriously. The sheep **might / can't** have died naturally; another animal (1) **can't / must** have killed them. We don't know what the animal was, but it (2) **can't / must** have been strong and dangerous. Someone saw a strange, black animal in the area, like a very large cat. It (3) **might / can't** have been a normal cat because it was too big and too fast. Police thought that the person (4) **might / can't** have made a mistake, but then other people saw it too. It is possible that this animal (5) **must / might** have killed the sheep. It was suggested that the animal (6) **might / can't** have escaped from a zoo. But a zoo (7) **must / might** have known if an animal had escaped, and no zoo has reported anything. The beast of Bodmin remains a mystery.

Criticising past actions: *should have*

3 Complete the sentences with *should* or *shouldn't*.

DOG KILLED BY BEAST OF BODMIN

The dog's owner *should* have been more careful.

1 He ...... have gone in the woods at night.
2 Someone ...... have told him that it was dangerous.
3 He ...... have taken his dog there after dark.
4 He ...... have listened to the newspaper's advice.
5 The police ...... have found the Beast of Bodmin by now.

Obligation and necessity

4 Complete the text with the correct form of *need to* or *have to*.

Before the Beast of Bodmin appeared, farmers *didn't need to* protect their sheep, but after the first attacks, people (**1**) ...... be more careful. Today, we still don't know what the Beast is, and we (**2**) ...... find out. We (**3**) ...... be frightened of the Beast because it's frightened of people. But it's dangerous to sheep, so the police (**4**) ...... catch it. Local hotels (**5**) ...... worry about business; lots of visitors go to Bodmin to look for the Beast!

5 Complete the sentences with *had to, didn't have to* or *wasn't / weren't allowed to*. Use the verbs in the box.

visit ~~go out~~ do stay in go stay up

Last night Paula's mum *had to go out.*

1 So Paula ...... to take care of her baby brothers.
2 She ...... her friend's house.
3 Her baby brothers ...... late because they are too young.
4 They ...... to bed at eight o'clock.
5 Paula ...... any homework, so she read her book *The Beast of Bodmin*.

The World of English 5

Round-up 5 (page 110)

Revision: **Reported speech, reported instructions, reported questions and question tags**

Function: **Phone messages**

1 Who has phoned Dave?

Culture File (page 112)

Topic: **The world of phones**

Vocabulary: **Abbreviations**

2 How many text messages are sent in Britain every year?

The Story of Pop (page 114)

Artist: **Fatboy Slim**

Type of music: **Dance**

Song: **Praise you**

3 Where was techno music developed?

Round-up 5

Reported speech

1 Write the questions and sentences in italics in reported speech.

"Are clothes important? (**1**) And *why do people think about clothes so much?* Well in my opinion (**2**) *they are because they are an important way of giving information about ourselves* to others. (**3**) *When we're walking down the street we look at people's faces, bodies and clothes.* (**4**) *We always look at people before we speak to them.* (**5**) *I met a boy who always wore jeans* and he had a lot of piercings in his ears and nose. Although he was a computer expert, he couldn't get a job because of the way he looked. Now, (**6**) *he has changed his image.* He is fashionable but smart and I'm sure (**7**) *he'll find a job.*"

1 He asked ....
2 He insisted ....
3 He explained..
4 He said ....
5 He told us ....
6 He explained..
7 He predicted ....

Question tags

2 Write the question tags.

Sandra: Hi, Nick. You've bought a new mobile phone, (**1**) .... you?

Nick: Yes, I dropped my old one and broke it.

Sandra: Wow! It looks nice (**2**) .... ?

Nick: You haven't got one, (**3**) .... you?

Sandra: No. I like speaking to people face to face! I must be strange, (**4**) .... ?

Nick: You don't like them, (**5**) .... ?

Sandra: I don't know. People can call you when they want, (**6**) .... ?

Nick: Yes, but what's wrong with that?

Sandra: I suppose I really like being alone! I also hate it when I'm speaking to someone and their mobile rings. They don't speak to you anymore, (**7**) .... ? It seems the mobile is more important!

Nick: Yes, you're right. Some people don't use them properly.

Possibility in the past

3 Complete the text.

may/might have **may/might not have** **must have** **can't have**

Books about the Bermuda Triangle say there (**1**) .... been some mysterious reason why planes and boats disappeared there. They claim these disappearances (**2**) .... all .... been accidents or because of bad weather. They think there (**3**) .... been other causes that cannot be easily explained.

The mystery began in 1945 when five airplanes from the US navy disappeared in the Atlantic ocean. The leader of the five planes was new to the area. The US navy say it is possible that he (**4**) .... got lost. He called on his radio, but communication was difficult and the US navy think he (**5**) .... understood very well. There was a storm in the Atlantic and some people are certain that the planes (**6**) .... crashed because of it. The problem is that the weather doesn't sell a lot of books!

Obligation, prohibition and necessity

4 Choose the correct word.

Last year, I visited the NASA space centre in Cape Canaveral in Florida with my family. When we arrived at NASA we (**1**) *had to/ weren't allowed to* have special identity cards made with our photos on them. We saw all the rockets and space shuttles that NASA are using now. Although there were lots of things to see, we (**2**) *weren't allowed to/ had to* take any photographs of the rockets and we (**3**) *didn't have to/ had to* leave our cameras and video cameras at the entrance. There were also some places we (**4**) *needed to/ weren't allowed to* visit because they were working on new space projects. We went on a space shuttle. I wanted to wear a space suit, but I (**5**) *didn't need to/ had to* because I wasn't in space! It was great sitting in the pilot's chair!

Listening

Phone messages

1 Complete the dialogue. Then listen and check.

phone message course sorry back
Bye calling Could speak speaking

Mary: Hello, Mary (**1**) ....
Tina: Oh, hello. Could I speak to Dave, please?
Mary: Just a minute. Who's (**2**) ....?
Tina: Tina.
Mary: Dave, it's Tina on the (**3**) ....
Dave: Tina! Say I'm not here!
Mary: What?
Dave: Say I've gone out!
Mary: I can't. I said you were here!
Dave: Please. I can't (**4**) .... to her now!
Mary: Tina? I'm (**5**) .... Dave isn't here. I didn't realize he'd gone out. Could I take a (**6**) .... ?
Tina: Oh. (**7**) .... you tell him I've got the photos?
Mary: You've got the photos. I'll tell him.
Tina: And could you ask him to phone me when he gets (**8**) ....?
Mary: Of (**9**) .... No problem!
Tina: Thanks. (**10**) ....
Mary: Bye. Dave, Tina's got the photos. Now, what's all this about?

Useful expressions

2 Find the expressions in the dialogue. What do they mean?

1 Speaking.
2 Could I take a message?
3 I didn't realize?
4 What's all this about?

3 Think of your information for a phone message. Use the ideas in pictures 1–4.

1 Could you tell Carmen ...

1 who . . .?
2 what . . .?
3 where . . .?
4 when . . .?

Dialogue

Phone messages

4 In pairs, discuss your ideas from exercise 3. Use the dialogue below as a model. Substitute the blue words to form your own dialogues.

A: Oh hello, it's Carmen here. Could I speak to Kate, please?
B: Sorry, Carmen, she isn't here at the moment. Can I take a message?
A: Oh, yes, could you tell her that I'll be at the café at six o'clock?
B: At the café at six. OK, I'll tell her. Bye Carmen.
A: Thanks a lot, bye.

Culture File 5

Texting

1 Work in pairs. Discuss the questions.

1. Do you ever use text messages?
2. What are the good and bad things about text messages?
3. Is there a special 'language' for text messages in your country?

2 Read the text. Then answer the questions.

1. How many years has SMS existed?
2. Why is SMS popular?
3. Where does text 'language' come from?
4. Does Jean Aitchison have a good opinion of text messages?
5. What is happening to text 'language' at the moment?

Vocabulary:
Text message abbreviations

3 Match phrases 1 – 10 with abbreviations a – j.

1 CUL8R
2 WKND
3 LO
4 RUOK
5 RUF2T
6 WAN2
7 PCM
8 THX
9 2DAY
10 GR8

a Thanks
b today
c weekend
d Hello!
e Are you OK?
f Great!
g See you later
h Are you free to talk?
i want to
j Please call me

Txt msgs

Text messages for mobile phones were introduced in January 1999. The service was called SMS ('Short Message Service') and it soon became very popular. Now approximately one billion text messages are sent every month in Britain alone. SMS is cheap and fast. It's good for companies because they can send information and adverts to clients. But most messages are sent by people who want to chat, or send silent or secret messages. A survey by Nokia showed that 64% of people flirted using SMS.

Young people send the most messages. In Britain, nearly 70% of fourteen to sixteen-year-olds have got a mobile phone or use their parents' mobiles. Teenager Fiona Sutton says, 'I sometimes send 30 messages a day - but not in class, honestly.' And Marco Miranda from London says, 'I first asked my girlfriend out with a text message. In fact the first month of our relationship survived only through text messages.' Marco's first invitation to his girlfriend was 'WD U LK 2 GO 4 A COFY?'

Text messages must be short, and Marco's invitation was typical of the text 'language' which has evolved from the informal style of e-mails. The language is still growing and you can now buy books with lists of abbreviations and symbols. Some experts think that this language is bad because it is not 'correct'. Jean Aitchison, from Oxford University, disagrees. She says, 'Over the past twenty years, language has changed very fast because of the way people use language with new technology. But this doesn't destroy the existing language, it adds to it.'

At the moment some people can't live without mobile phones and text messages. We will have to wait and see how they change our lives and languages.

4 **Listen to the story of texting and TV in the USA. Put the events in the correct order.**

a More Americans learned to send text messages. 1 ......

b A new TV show asked people to vote. 2 ......

c Americans don't like text messages. 3 ......

d A game is created. 4 ......

Did you know?

- Scientists started researching mobile phone technology in the 1940s.
- There is not one standard system for mobile phones in the USA.
- Local phone calls from land-line phones are free in the USA, so people prefer to use them or use email.

5 **Listen to the text again. Are the sentences true or false?**

1 SMS was popular in China in 2003. ....

2 The average American mobile phone user sent 13 texts a month. ....

3 *American Idol* is a TV talent competition. ....

4 In May 2003, most people who sent a text message to the show hadn't used SMS before. ....

5 The third series of the show created more SMS users. ....

Project

How do your classmates and family communicate? Ask people about the means of communication in the box. Why do they use them? How often do they use them? And what are the advantages of different methods of communication?

telephone mobile phone e-mail
letter fax notes post cards

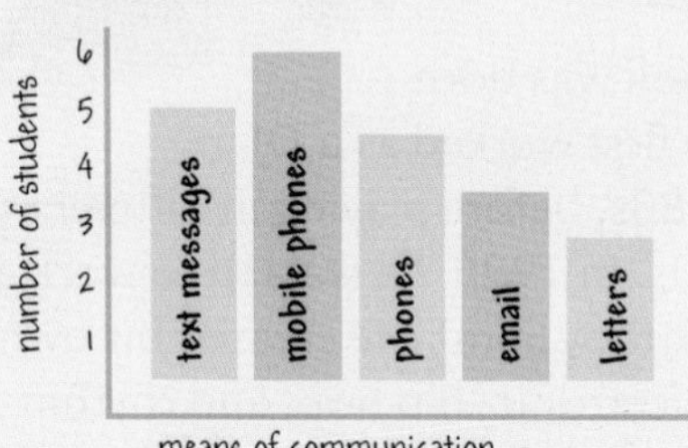

Find the results and draw a graph.

The Story of Pop 5

Dance

1 Read and listen. Then answer the questions.

1 When and where did 'house' music originate?
2 Did 'techno' music come from the same place as house music?
3 When did Norman Cook first start to work as a DJ?
4 What type of music does Fatboy Slim make?
5 What are the characteristics of 'big beat' music?

2 Put the words in the correct order. Then listen and check.

We've come a long, long way together.

Praise you

a and the good.
b you baby.
c a long, long way
d Through the hard times
e I have
f like I should.
g I have to praise you
h together.
i to celebrate
j We've come

Dance

Modern dance music has evolved from a lot of different styles. DJs in Chicago in the 1980s started to compose electronic 'house' music using synthesizers, drum and bass machines, and other electronic equipment. House music often included 'samples' (short pieces) of jazz, rap, soul and reggae.

'Techno', another type of electronic dance music, was developed in Detroit. From techno and house music, many different styles have evolved, including: acid house, jungle and hard-core. Hard-core is the fastest style of house music – it's got more than 160 beats per minute!

Fatboy Slim

Norman Cook was born in 1963. He first worked as a DJ in the early 1980s, before playing in different pop groups in the '80s and '90s. In 1996, he started to work again as a DJ, using the name 'Fatboy Slim'. He created his own music from a mixture of electronic, hip hop, and rhythm and blues. In 2000, Fatboy Slim was Britain's most popular 'big beat' artist. Big beat is a combination of rhythm and blues, techno and hip hop.

Grammar

Unit 1

Present simple

Affirmative		Negative	
I *You	speak	I You	don't speak
He She It	speaks	He She It	doesn't speak
We They	speak	We They	don't speak

*NB the singular and plural form of the verb following *you* are always the same

Questions

Do	I / you	speak ...?
Does	he / she / it	speak ...?
Do	we / they	speak ...?

Present continuous

Affirmative		Negative	
I	'm talking	I	'm not talking
You	're talking	You	aren't talking
He She It	's talking	He She It	isn't talking
We They	're talking	We They	aren't talking

'm = am 're = are 's = is

Questions

Am	I	talking ...?
Are	you	talking ...?
Is	he / she / it	talking ...?
Are	we / they	talking ...?

Present simple and present continuous

- **We use the present simple to talk about routines.**
  What *do* you *read?* I normally *read* comics.
- **We use the present continuous to talk about an action that is happening at the moment.**
  What *are* you *reading* at the moment?
  I'*m reading* a book.

Past simple

Affirmative		Negative	
I / You He / She / It We / They	saw	I / You He / She / It We / They	didn't see

Questions

Did	I / you he / she / it we / they	see ...?

Past continuous

Affirmative		Negative	
I	was sleeping	I	wasn't sleeping
You	were sleeping	You	weren't sleeping
He She It	was sleeping	He She It	wasn't sleeping
We They	were sleeping	We They	weren't sleeping

Questions

Was	I	sleeping ...?
Were	you	sleeping ...?
Was	he / she / it	sleeping ...?
Were	we / they	sleeping ...?

Past simple and past continuous

- **We use the past simple to describe:**
- **a finished action in the past.**
  My watch *stopped* at 9.15.
- **states in the past.**
  We *were* scared.
- **the progress of an action in the past.**
  I *was watching* TV yesterday morning.
- **We can use the past simple and the past continuous in the same sentence. We use the past continuous to describe the longer action. We use the past simple to describe the interruption.**
  I *was watching* TV when my watch *stopped*

Past perfect

Affirmative		Negative	
I / You He / She / It We / They	'd seen had seen	I / You He / She / It We / They	hadn't seen

'd = had

- **We use the past perfect to talk about an action in the past, which happened before another action in the past.**
  When he*'d finished* his homework, he went out.
  OR
  He went out when *he'd finished* his homework.
  (First action: he finished his homework. Second action: he went out.)

used to

Affirmative

I / You He / She / It We / They	used to go swimming. used to have long hair.

Negative

I / You He / She / It We / They	didn't use to go swimming. didn't use to have long hair.

Questions

Did	I / you / he / she / it we / they	use to go swimming?

- **We use *used to* + verb to describe a habit or a state in the past.**
  I *used to play* football every day.
  He *used to be* friendly.

ago

- **We use *ago* to talk about when something took place in the past. *Ago* refers to the time between the event and now.**
  That was 11 years *ago*.

Unit 2

Present perfect simple

Affirmative		Negative	
I You	've arrived	I You	haven't arrived
He She It	's arrived	He She It	hasn't arrived
We They	've arrived	We They	haven't arrived

've = have 's = has

Questions

Have	I / you	arrived ... ?
Has	he / she / it	arrived ... ?
Have	we / they	arrived ... ?

- **We use the present perfect to talk about experiences in our lives.**
  I*'ve been* to America.
  I*'ve* never *read* a book in Italian.
- ***Ever* means in *your life*.**
  Have you *ever* driven a car?

Present perfect with *for* and *since*

for	*since*
a minute	1986
a few hours	June
months and months	yesterday
a hundred years	Monday

- **We use *for* with periods of time. *For* tells us about the length of time of the action.**
  I've been here *for* three days.
- **We use *since* with points in time. *Since* tells us when an action started.**
  He's lived in London *since* 1999.

Present perfect and past simple

- **We use the present perfect to talk about an action that started in the past, when the time period is not finished or the time is not specified.**

  I*'ve lived* in Huelva since 1999. (I live in Huelva now.)

  I*'ve lived* in Paris, Rome and London. (The listener doesn't know when.)

- **We use the past simple with a completed action in the past.**

  I *lived* in Madrid between 1997 and 1999.

Present perfect continuous

Affirmative

I You	've been waiting
He She It	's been waiting
We They	've been waiting

Negative

I You	haven't been waiting
He She It	hasn't been waiting
We They	haven't been waiting

Questions

Have	I / you	been waiting ...?
Has	he / she / it	been waiting ...?
Have	we / they	been waiting ...?

- **We use the present perfect continuous for an action or repeated actions that started in the past and continued to the present.**

  I*'ve been playing* tennis since I was six.

- **We use it to emphasis the activity and the length of the activity.**

  I*'ve been waiting* for you for an hour.

Unit 3

will

Affirmative

I / You He / She / It We / They	'll be happy will

'll = will

Negative

I / You He / She / It We / They	won't be happy

won't = will not

Questions

Will	I / you he / she / it we / they	be happy?

- **We use *will* for predictions about the future.**

  I think that she*'ll* be happy.

going to

Affirmative

I	'm going to play
You	're going to play
He / She / It	's going to play
We / They	're going to play

Negative

I	'm not going to play
You	aren't going to play
He / She / It	isn't going to play
We / They	aren't going to play

Questions

Am	I	going to play ...?
Are	you	going to play ...?
Is	he / she / it	going to play ...?
Are	we / they	going to play ...?

- **We use *going to* to talk about plans and intentions in the future.**

  She*'s going to* start a new job soon.

Present continuous

- **We use the present continuous for arrangements in the future.**

  I*'m meeting* my aunt for lunch next week.

Present simple

- **We use the present simple for timetables and schedules.**
  My school *starts* at eight every morning.

First conditional

- **We use the first conditional to talk about actions and their probable consequences.**
- **In one clause we use *if* + present simple. This clause describes an action.**
  If I *see* Linda, ...
- **In the other clause, we use *will* or *won't* + infinitive. This clause describes a probable consequence of the action.**
  ... I'*ll say* 'Hello'.
- **We can reverse the order of the clauses.**
  If I *see* Linda, I'*ll say* 'Hello'.
  I'*ll say* 'Hello' if I *see* Linda.

before, *when* and *after*

- **We do not use *will* following *before*, *when* or *after*. To refer to the future we use the present simple or present perfect with these words. We can use the present simple with all of them and the present perfect with *when* and *after*.**
  When I *have* my own home, I'll get a dog.
  I'm going to the cinema *when* I'*ve finished* my homework.

Unit 4

Second conditional

- **We use the second conditional to talk about a theoretical situation.**
- **In one clause, we use *if* + past simple. This clause describes a situation that is unreal at the moment.**
  If I *had* more money, ...
- **In the other clause, we use *would* + infinitive. This clause describes a possible consequence of the situation.**
  ... I'*d buy* a car.

Third Conditional

- **We use the third conditional to talk about actions and consequences in the past.**
- **In one clause, we use *if* + past perfect. This clause describes a situation in the past that didn't happen.**
  If you *had told* me it was a secret, ... (You didn't tell me a secret.)
- **In the other clause, we use *would* / *wouldn't have* + infinitive. This clause describes a possible result of the situation in the past.**
  ...I *wouldn't have* repeated it.

too, *so* and *such*

- ***too*, *so* and *such* are used for emphasis.**
- ***too* = more than necessary.**
  Those boots are *too* expensive.
- ***so* and *such* are often used to make a positive adjective more positive.**
  He was *so* nice. He's *such* a nice person.
- ***too* and *so* can be used before an adjective or adverb.**
  The boots were *too* expensive. They were *so* expensive that I couldn't buy them.
- ***such* is used before *a/an* + adjective + noun.**
  It was *such* a good film.

Unit 5

Possibility: *may* / *might*, *must* and *can't*

- **are modal verbs. Modal verbs are all followed by an infinitive without *to*.**
  She *must like* you.
  NOT: ~~She *must to like* you~~.

may / *might*

Affirmative

I / You He / She / It We / They	may / might go

Negative

I / You He / She / It We / They	may / might not go

Questions

May	I / you	
	he / she / it	go?
Might	we / they	

- **We can use *may* or *might* to talk about something which is possible but not certain.**

  I *may* be late tomorrow.

  Jim *might not* understand the question.

- ***may* and *might* have a similar meaning.**

  I *may* be late. = I *might* be late.

must and *can't*

Affirmative

I / You He / She / It We / They	must like trees

Negative

I / You He / She / It We / They	can't be very old

- **We can use *must* and *can't* to talk about things we are certain about.**

  Your picture *must* be a copy.

  It *can't* be the original picture.

- **When we talk about probability, we use *must* in affirmative sentences and *can't* in negative sentences.**

  The lights are on. They *must* be at home.

  The lights are off. They *can't* be at home.

  NOT: ~~They *mustn't* be at home~~.

Ability: *can* and *could*

Present

Affirmative	
I / You He / She / It We / They	can swim
Negative	
I / You He / She / It We / They	can't swim

Past

Affirmative	
I / You He / She / It We / They	could read
Negative	
I / You He / She / It We / They	couldn't read

- **We use *can* and *could* to talk about abilities and skills in the present and the past.**
- ***could* is the past of *can*.**
- **We use *can* and *could* + verb, without *to*.**

  I *couldn't go* out. NOT: ~~I *couldn't to go* out~~.

Obligation: *have to* and *had to*

Present

Affirmative		Negative	
I You	have to study	I You	don't have to study
He She It	has to study	He She It	doesn't have to study
We They	have to study	We They	don't have to study

Past

Affirmative	
I / You He / She / It We / They	had to study
Negative	
I / You He / She / It We / They	didn't have to study

- **We use affirmative forms of *have to* and *had to* when we talk about obligation in the present and in the past.**

  I *had to* go. (I was obliged to go.)

- **We use negative forms when there is not an obligation to do anything.**

  I *didn't have to go*. (It wasn't necessary.)

Unit 6

Gerunds

- **A gerund is the *-ing* form of a verb. We can use the gerund as the subject of a sentence.**
  Smoking is unhealthy.

The infinitive of purpose

- **We sometimes use *to* + infinitive to explain why we do something.**
  I phoned you *to tell* you the news.

Gerunds and infinitives

- **We also use a gerund after verbs of preference, for example *like*, *love*, *enjoy*, *don't mind* and *hate*.**
  I *love* reading. I *hate* washing up.
- **We also use *to* + infinitive after verbs of intention, for example *promise*, *plan*, *agree*, *want* and *try*.**
  I promised *to help*.

Unit 7

Relative clauses: *who*, *which* and *that*

- **We use relative clauses to give important information about a noun.**
- **We use the relative pronouns *who*, *which* and *that* to form relative clauses. We do not use a subject pronoun in the relative clause.**
  The Police are looking for the man *who* stole the money.
  NOT: ~~The Police are looking for the man *who* he stole the money~~.
- **We can use *which* or *that* with things.**
  I stayed in a hotel *which* / *that* was really old.
- **We can use *who* or *that* with people.**
  There are lots of people *who* / *that* want to try it.

Articles: *a* / *an*, *the* and *no article*

a / *an*

- **We use *a* / *an* with singular countable nouns when we first mention them.**
  I saw *a* film last night.

the

- **We use *the* with singular, plural and uncountable nouns.**
- **We also use *the* when we mention a specific thing or things again.**
- **We can use *the* when the context tells us which specific thing or things we mean.**
  The man you were talking to is my uncle.
- **We use *the* when there is only one of them.**
  The first man on *the* moon was Neil Armstrong.
- **We use *the* with countries that have States, Kingdom or Republic in their names.**
  The United States of America, *The* United Kingdom
- **We use *the* with oceans, seas, mountains, deserts and rivers.**
  The Baltic Sea, *The* Thames

no article

- **We use *no article* when we talk about things generally.**
  I like playing computer games.
- **We use *no article* with most countries.**
  I went to Spain.

Unit 8

Present simple passive

Affirmative		Negative	
I	'm taught	I	'm not taught
You	're taught	You	aren't taught
He She It	's taught	He She It	isn't taught
We They	're taught	We They	aren't taught

'm = am 're = are 's = is

Questions

Am	I	taught ...?
Are	you	taught ...?
Is	he / she / it	taught ...?
Are	we / they	taught ...?

Past simple passive

Affirmative		**Negative**	
I	was taught	I	wasn't taught
You	were taught	You	weren't taught
He She It	was taught	He She It	wasn't taught
We They	were taught	We They	weren't taught

Questions

Was	I	taught ...?
Were	you	taught ...?
Was	he / she / it	taught ...?
Were	we / they	taught ...?

The passive (present and past simple)

- **We use the passive when we want to emphasize the action and not the person or the thing that does the action.**
  Active: They *make* CDs in Japan.
  Passive: CDs *are made* in Japan.
  Active: They *translated* the book.
  Passive: The book *was translated*.

by

- **We use *by* when we want to mention the agent.**
  Active: Baird invented TV in 1924.
  Passive: TV was invented *by* Baird in 1924.

Causative: *have* (*have something done*)

Affirmative		**Negative**	
I You	have the car fixed	I You	don't have the car fixed
He She It	has the car fixed	He She It	doesn't have the car fixed
We They	have the car fixed	We They	don't have the car fixed

Questions

Do	I / you / we / they	have the car fixed ...?
Does	he / she / it	have the car fixed ...?

- **We use the causative *have* when people don't do the action themselves, but somebody does it for them. They usually do it for money.**
  I *had* my hair *cut* yesterday.

Unit 9

Reported speech

Direct speech	**Reported speech**
Present simple	Past simple
'It **looks** great!'	He said that it **looked** great.
Present continuous	Past continuous
'I'**m listening**.'	She said that she **was listening**.
Past simple	Past perfect
'I **saw** the film.'	She said that she'**d seen** the film.
Present perfect	Past perfect
'He'**s seen** us.'	I said that he'**d seen** us.
will	*would*
'This **will** help.'	He said that this **would** help.
can	*could*
'It **can't** see us.'	She said that it **couldn't** see us.

- **When we report what someone said, the verb tenses change and the pronouns and possessive adjectives usually change.**
  'I'm waiting for my friend'
  He said he was waiting for his friend.

Reported instructions

- **We use *tell* + object pronoun + infinitive to report instructions.**
  'Be quiet.' *He told me to be quiet.*

Reported questions

- **When we report a question, we don't use a question mark.**
  'How was your weekend?'
  He asked me how my weekend had been.
  NOT:
  ~~*He asked me how my weekend had been?*~~
- **When we report a question, we change the word order of the question.**
  'Where are you?'
  They asked me where I was.
  NOT: ~~*They asked me where was I.*~~
- **We use *if* or *whether* when we report a yes / no question**
  'Did you see him?'
  He asked me *if / whether* I had seen him.

Questions tags

- **We use the correct auxiliary verb (*do*, *be*, *have*, *can*) to make the question tag.**
  You like it, *don't you*?
  You're from Gdansk, *aren't you*?
  You've done it before, *haven't you*?
  You can swim, *can't you*?
- **When the first part of the sentence is affirmative, the question tag is negative. When the first part of the sentence is negative, the question tag is affirmative.**
  You *will* tell him, *won't you*?
  You *aren't* happy, *are you*?

Unit 10

Possibility in the past: *may / might*, *must* and *can't*

- **We can use *may* or *might* (+ *not*) + *have* + past participle to talk about something which is possible but not certain in the past.**
  She *may have made* a mistake.
  He *may not have* heard you.
  I *might have looked* at the flowers.
  He *might not have* remembered.
- ***may* + *have* and *might* + *have* have a similar meaning.**
  I *may have* = I *might have*
- **When we talk about probability in the past, we use *must* + *have* in affirmative sentences and *can't* + *have* in negative sentences.**
  The lights were on last night. They *must have been* at home.
  The lights were off last night. They *can't have been* at home.
  NOT: ~~They *mustn't have* been at home.~~
- ***May / might*, *must* and *can't* are modal verbs. Modal verbs are all followed by an infinitive without *to*.**
  She *must have told* you.
  NOT: ~~She *must to have told* you.~~

may + have

Affirmative

I / You He / She / It We / They	may have gone

Negative

I / You He / She / It We / They	may not have gone

might + have

Affirmative

I / You He / She / It We / They	might have gone

Negative

I / You He / she / it We / They	might not have gone

must + have

I / You He / she / it We / They	must have gone

can't + have

I / You He / She / It We / They	can't have gone

Criticising past actions: *should have*

Affirmative

I / You He / She / It We / They	should have asked her name.

Negative

I / You He / She / It We / They	shouldn't have asked her name.

Question

Should	I / you / he / she / it we / they	have asked her name?

- **We can use *should have* + past participle to criticise something that didn't happen in the past.**
  I *should have studied* harder for my exams.

- **We can use *should not have* + past participle to criticise something that happened in the past.**
  I'm tired. I *shouldn't have stayed* up so late last night.

Obligation, necessity and prohibition: *need to*, *have to* and *be allowed to*

present	past
have / has to must	had to
have / has to must need to	had to needed to
don't / doesn't have to don't / doesn't need to mustn't not be allowed to	didn't have to didn't need to wasn't / weren't allowed to

Obligation: *must* and *have to*

- **We can use *must* or *have / has to* to talk about something we are obliged to do.**
  I *had* to do my homework.

No obligation: *don't have to* and *don't need to*

- **We use negative forms of *have / has to* or *need to* when there is not an obligation to do anything.**
  I *didn't have to* go to town. = I *didn't need to* go to town.

Necessity: *have to* and *need to*

- **We can use *have / has to, must* or *need to* to talk about necessity without obligation.**
  I *need to* buy some shampoo.

Prohibition: *mustn't* and *not be allowed to*

- **We can use *mustn't* and *not be allowed to* when there is an obligation not to do something.**
  I'm *not allowed* to borrow my father's car.

Vocabulary

Unit 1

1.1 Periods adjectives

1960s /ˈnaɪnti:n ˈsɪksti:z/
ancient /ˈeɪnʃənt/
bronze-age /ˈbrɒnzeɪdʒ/
fifteenth-century /fɪfti:nθ ˈsentʃəri/
medieval /medjˈi:vəl/
modern /ˈmɒdɜ:(r)n
prehistoric /prihəsˈtɒrɪk/
Victorian /vɪkˈtəʊrjɪən/

1.2 Periods of time

century /ˈsentʃəri/
day /deɪ/
decade /ˈdekeɪd/
hour /ˈaʊə(r)/
millennium /mɪˈleniəm/
minute /ˈmɪnɪt/
month /mʌnθ/
morning /ˈmɔ:(r)nɪŋ/
second /ˈsekənd/
week /wi:k/
weekend /wɪˈkend/
year /jɪə(r)/

1.3 Other nouns

beach /bi:tʃ/
birth /bɜ:θ/
botanist /bɒtənɪst/
bowl /bəʊl/
building /ˈbɪldɪŋ/
bus stop /ˈbʌs stɒp/
camera /kæmərə/
candle /ˈkændəl/
Christian /ˈkrɪstʃɪn/
civilisation /sɪvɪlaɪzˈeɪʃən/
coach /kəʊtʃ/
Colosseum /kɒləˈsi:əm/
combination /kɒmbɪˈneɪn/
crew /kru:/
date /deɪt/
discovery /dɪˈskʌvəri/
Dutchman /ˈdʌtʃmən/
Egyptian /ˈɪ:dʒɪpʃn/
engineer /endʒɪˈnɪ(r)/
exam result /ɪgˈzæm rɪˌzʌlt/
general knowledge /ˈdʒenrəl ˈnɒlɪdʒ/
genius /ˈdʒi:njəs/
glasses /ˈglæsɪs/
Greek /gri:k/
guide /gaɪd/
harvest /ˈhɑ:vɪst/
idea /aɪˈdɪə/
journey /ˈdʒɜ:ni/
king /kɪŋ/
knot /n ɑt/
list /lɪst/
memory /ˈmeməri/
mental block /ˈmentl blok/
model /ˈmɒdəl/
moon /mu:n/
myth /mɪθ/
nature /neɪtʃə/
obelisk /ˈɒbəlɪsk/
object /ˈɒbdʒekt/
officer /ˈɒfisə/
opinion /əˈpɪnjɪn/
origin /ˈɒrɪdʒɪn/
period /pɪərɪ:əd/
pilgrim /ˈpɪlgrɪm/
place /pleɪs/
present /ˈprezənt/
priest /pri:st/
prize /praɪz/
problem /ˈprɒbləm/
programme /ˈprəʊgræm/
psychologist /saɪˈkɒlədʒɪst/
relative /ˈrelətɪv/
reunion /ri:ˈju:niən/
sample /ˈsɑ:mpl/
scientist /ˈsaɪəntɪst/
servant /ˈsɜ:vənt/
sign /saɪn/
star /stɑ:(r)/
stick /stɪk/
string /strɪŋ/
suggestion /sʌˈdʒestjən/
tradition /trəˈdɪʃn/
trip /trɪp/
type /taɪp/
uniform /ju:nəfɔ:(r)m/
watch /wɒtʃ/
yo-yo /ˈjəʊjəʊ/

1.4 Verbs

arrive /əˈraɪv/
become /bəˈkʌm/
build /bɪld/
call /kɔ:l/
chat /tʃæt/
choose /tʃu:z/
collect /kəˈlekt/
control /kənˈtrəʊl/
count /kaʊnt/
cry /kraɪ/
decide /dəˈsaɪd/
decorate /ˈdekəreɪt/
die /daɪ/
dream /dri:m/
enjoy /ɪnˈdʒɔɪ/
explore /eksˈplɔ:(r)/
feed /fi:d/
finish /ˈfɪnɪʃ/
follow /ˈfɒləʊ/
forget /fə(r)ˈget/
go down /gəʊ ˈdaʊn/
guess /ges/
hate /heɪt/
imagine /ˈɪmædʒin/
improve /ɪmˈpru:v/
include /ɪnˈklu:d/
invent /ɪnˈvent/
invite /ɪnˈvaɪt/
laugh /lɑ:f/
leave /li:v/
need /ni:d/
offer /ˈɒfə(r)/
raise /reɪz/
realize /ˈriəlaɪz/
remember /rəˈmembə(r)/
replace /rɪˈpleɪs/
reply /rɪˈplaɪ/
ring /rɪŋ/
stay awake /steɪ əˈweɪk/
surprise /səˈpraɪz/
travel /ˈtrævl/
turn off /tɜ:(r)n ˈɒf/
wait /weɪt/
wear /weə(r)/
win /wɪn/

1.5 Adjectives

awful /ˈɔ:fəl/
clever /ˈklevə(r)/
crazy /ˈkreɪzi/
Dutch /dʌtʃ/
early /ˈɜ:li/
exciting /əkˈsaɪtɪŋ/
fantastic /fənˈtæstɪk/
hard /hɑ:d/
important /ɪmˈpɔ:tənt/
interesting /ˈɪntrəstɪŋ/
loud /laʊd/
national /ˈnæʃnəl/
nervous /ˈnɜ:vəs/
official /əˈfɪʃl/
pagan /ˈpeɪgən/
poor /pʊə(r)/
popular /ˈpɒpjələ(r)/
powerful /ˈpaʊ(ər)fəl/
recent /ˈri:sənt/
Roman /ˈrəʊmən/
scientific /saɪənˈtɪfɪk/
shy /ʃaɪ/
strange /streɪndʒ/
wise /waɪz/

1.6 Adverbs

ago /əˈgəʊ/
sometimes /ˈsʌmtaɪmz/.
usually /ˈju:ʒəli/

Unit 2

2.1 Romantic gifts
aftershave /'ɑ:ftəʃeɪv/
box of chocolates /bɒks əv 'tʃɒkləts/
bunch of flowers /bʌntʃ əv 'flaʊəz/
CD of love songs /si: di: əv 'lʌv sɒŋz/
cuddly toy /kʌdli 'tɔɪ/
love letter /'lʌv letə(r)/
perfume /'pɜ:fju:m/
poetry book /'pəʊətri bʊk/
ring /rɪŋ/
romantic card /rəʊmæntɪk 'kɑ:d/
romantic novel /rəʊmæntɪk 'nɒvl/
silver chain /sɪlvə 'tʃeɪn/
ticket for the cinema /tɪkɪt fə ðə 'sɪnəmə/

2.2 Horoscopes
Aquarius /ə'kweəriəs/
Aries /'eəri:z/
Cancer /'kænsə(r)/
Capricorn /'kæprɪkɔ:n/
Gemini /'dʒemɪnaɪ/
Leo /'li:əʊ/
Libra /'li:brə/
Pisces /'paɪsi:z/
Sagittarius /sædʒɪ'teəriəs/
Scorpio /'skɔ:piəʊ/
Taurus /'tɔ:rəs/
Virgo /'vɜ:gəʊ/

2.3 Relationships
ask someone out /ɑ:sk sʌmwʌn 'aʊt/
fall in love with someone /fɔ:l ɪn lʌv wɪð 'sʌmwʌn/
get engaged to someone /get ɪn'geɪdʒd tə sʌmwʌn/
get married to someone /get 'mæri:d tə sʌmwʌn/
go out with someone /gəʊ 'aʊt wɪð sʌmwʌn/
have an argument with someone /hæv ən 'ɑ:gjumənt wɪð sʌmwʌn/
meet someone /'mi:t sʌmwʌn/
split up with someone /splɪt 'ʌp wɪð sʌmwʌn/

2.4 Other nouns
accident /'æksɪdənt/
advice /əd'vaɪs/
anniversary /ænɪ'vɜ:səri/
arrange /əreɪndʒ/
attraction /ə'trækʃn/
consequence /'kɒnsɪkwens/
couple /'kʌpl/
diamond /'daɪmənd/
divorce /dɪ'vɔ:s/
engaged /ɪn'geɪdʒd/
fan /fæn/
fisherman /'fɪʃə(r)mən/
gift /gɪft/
goddess /'gɒdes/
gold /gəʊld/
ingredient /ɪn'gri:djɪnt/
letter /letə(r)/
lip /lɪp/
love potion /'lʌv pəʊʃn/
magazine /mægə'zi:n/
marriage /'mærɪdʒ/
message /'mæsɑ:ʒ/
motorbike /'məʊtəbaɪk/
partner /'pɑ:(r)tnə(r)/
possession /pə'zeʃɪn/
reserve /rɪ'zɜ:v/
rhino /'raɪnəʊ/
soldier /'səʊldʒə(r)/
superstition /sʊpə(r)'stɪʃən/
tiger /'taɪgə(r)/
Valentine card /'væləntaɪn kɑ:d/
Venus /'vi:nəs/
verse /vɜ:s/
voice /vɔis/
wife /waɪf/
wood /wu:d/

2.5 Verbs
break /breɪk/
discover /dɪs'kʌvə(r)/
drop /drɒp/
estimate /'estɪmət/
explain /eks'pleɪn/
fear /'fɪə(r)/
feel /fi:l/
hunt /hʌnt/
kiss /kɪs/
mend /mend/
reach /ri:tʃ/
respect /rəs'pekt/
smile /smaɪl/
symbolize /'sɪmbəlaɪz/
throw /θrəʊ/
wish /wɪʃ/

2.6 Adjectives
bright /braɪt/
calm /cɑ:m/
careful /'keɪ(r)fəl/
compatible /kəm'pætɪbl/
cruel /krʊəl/
exotic /eg'zɒtɪk/
frequent /'fri:kwənt/
good-looking /gu:d 'lu:kɪŋ/
lovely /'lʌvli/
perfect /'pɜ:(r)fəkt/
romantic /rə'mæntɪk/
serious /'sɪərɪəs/
special /'speʃəl/
strict /strɪkt/
superstitious /su:pə'stɪʃəs/
traditional /trɪ'dɪʃənəl/

2.7 Adverbs
curiously /'kjuəriəsli/
particularly /pə'tɪkjələ(r)li/
recently /'ri:sɪntli/
twice /twaɪs/
unfortunately /ʌn'fɔɪ(r)tʃʊnətli/

Unit 3

3.1 World Issues
animal rights /ænɪml 'raɪts/
disease /dɪ'zi:z/
famine /'fæmɪn/
genetic engineering /dʒənetɪk endʒɪ'nɪərɪŋ/
immigration /ɪmɪ'greɪʃn/
poverty /'pɒvə(r)ti/
terrorism /'terərɪzəm/
the environment /di: ɪn'vaɪrəmənt/
war /wɔ:(r)/

3.2 Other nouns
AIDS /eɪdz/
air pollution /eə pə'lu:ʃən/
apathy /'æpəθi/
appeal /ə'pi:l/
banner /'bænə(r)/
boycott /'bɔɪkɒt/
burden /'bɜ:dn/
campaign /kæm'peɪn/
cell /sel/
cereal /'si:rjɪəl/
characteristic /kærɪktə'rɪstɪk/
charity /'tʃærəti/
chemical /'kemɪkəl/
climate /'klaɪmɪt/
clone /kləʊn/
collection box /kə'lekʃn bɒks/
company /'kʌmpəni/
concert /'kɒnsə(r)t/
danger /'deɪndʒə(r)/
debate /dɪ'beɪt/
demonstration /demən'streɪʃn/
desert /'dezɜ:(r)t/

developing world /dıveləpıŋ 'wɜ:ld/
doctor /'dɒktə(r)/
drug /drʌg/
dump /dʌmp/
Earth /ɜ:(r)θ/
ecologist /ı'kɒlədʒıst/
election /ı'lekʃn/
emergency /ı'mɜ:dʒənsi/
energy /'enədʒi/
epidemic /epı'demık/
farm animal /fɑ:(r)m ænıməl/
gang /gæŋ/
gene /dʒi:n/
global warming /'gləʊbəl wɔ:(r)mıŋ/
government /'gʌvəmənt/
guest /gest/
ignorance /'ıgnərəns/
instruction /ın'strʌkʃən/
leaflet /'li:flət/
malaria /mə'leıri:ə/
marathon /'mæræθən/
material /mə'tıeriəl/
mutation /mju:'teıʃən/
organisation /ɒrgınaız'eıʃən/
organism /'ɒrgənısəm/
orphan /'ɔ:fən/
peace /pi:s/
petition /pə'tıʃn/
politician /pɒlı'tıʃın/
placard /'plækɑ:d/
poster /'pəʊstə(r)/
prediction /prı'dıkʃən/
prejudice /'predʒʊdıs/
presenter /prə'sentə(r)/
priority /praı'ɒrəti/
recycling /rə'saıklıŋ/
responsibility /rıspɒnsı'bılıti/
route /ru:t/
rubbish dump /'rʌbıʃ dʌmp/
rule /ru:l/
security guard /sı'kjʊrıti ga:(r)d/
shanty town /'ʃænti taʊn/
situation /sıtʃʊ'eıʃən/
slogan /'sləʊgən/
species /'spi:ʃi:z/
sticker /'stıkə(r)/
stuff /stʌf/
support /sə'pɔ:(r)t/
temperature /'temprətʃə(r)/
term /tɜ:m/
university /ju:nı'vɜ:(r)sıti/
vegetarian /vedʒı'teıri:jən/
victim /'vıktım/
virus /'vaırʌs/
wing /wıŋ/

3.3 Verbs

change /tʃeındʒ/
contact /'kɒntækt/
continue /kən'tınjʊ/
create /kri'jeıt/
donate /də'neıt/
duplicate /'d(j)ʊplıkeıt/
eliminate /ı'lımıneıt/
experiment /eks'perımənt/
happen /'hæpən/
hurt /hʌ(r)t/
increase /ın'kri:s/
infect /ın'fekt/
inherit /ın'herıt/
make progress /meık 'prəʊgres/
manipulate /mə'nıpjəleıt/
modify /'mɒdıfaı/
organize /'ɔ:rgənaız/
predict /prə'dıkt/
promise /'prɒmıs/
protect /prə'tekt/
resist /rə'zıst/
respond /rı'spɒnd/
save /seıv/
specialize /'speʃəlaız/
spend /spend/
sponsor /'sponsə(r)/
sponsor money /'sponsə mʌni/
suffer /'sʌfə(r)/
survive /sə'vaıv/

3.4 Adjectives

abandoned /ə'bændənd/
angry /'ængri/
dying /'daıjıŋ/
effective /ı'fektıv/
emotional /ı'məʊʃınəl/
extinct /ık'stıŋkt/
illegal /ı'li:gəl/
immense /ı'mens/
moving /'mu:vıŋ/
resistant /rızıstənt/
right /raıt/
sponsored /'spɒnsəd/
tropical /'trɒpıkəl/

Unit 4

4.1 Body Art

contact lenses /'kɒntækt lenzız/
cosmetic surgery /kɒzmetık 'sɜ:dʒəri/
hairstyle /'heəstaıl/
jewellery /'dʒu:lri/
make-up /'meıkʌp/
piercing /'pıəsıŋ/
tattoo /tæ'tu:/
wig /wıg/

4.2 Other nouns

anorexia /ænə'reksiə/
appearance /ə'peərəns/
beauty spot /bju:ti spɒt
body /'bɒdi/
bulimia /bə'li:miə/
business executive /'bıznəs ekˌsekjətıv/
castle /'kɑ:səl/
catalogue /'kætəlɒg/
client /'klaıənt/
corset /'kɔ:sıt/
credit card /'kredıt kɑ:(r)d/
eating disorder /'i:tıŋ dısɔ:də(r)/
everybody /'evribɒdi/
fashion victim /'fæʃn vıktım/
female /'fi:meıl/
height /haıt/
hypothesis /haı'pɒθəsıs/
image consultant /'ımıdʒ kənsʌltənt/
interview /'ıntə(r)vju:/
invention /ın'venʃən/
jacket /'dʒækət/
knee /ni:/
pain /peın/
platform shoe /plætfɔ:m 'ʃu:/
shape /ʃeıp/
skin /skın/
slave /sleıv/
statistic /stə'tıstık/
tongue /tʌng/
tribe /traıb/
trousers /'traʊzə(r)z/
weight /weıt/

4.3 Verbs

analyse /'ænəlaız/
arrange /ə'reınʒ/
identify /aı'dentıfaı/
influence /'ınflʊəns/
lose weight /lu:z 'weıt/
put on /pʊt 'ɒn/
suit /su:t/

4.4 Other adjectives

alternative /ɒl'tɜ:(r)nətıv/
attractive /ə'træktıv/
badly dressed /bædli 'drest/
baggy /'bægi/
bored /bɔ:(r)d/
boring /'bəʊrıŋ/
cheap /tʃi:p/
comfortable /'kʌmftəbəl/
confident /'kɒnfıdənt/
cream /kri:m/
creative /kri'eıtıv/
designer-label /dızaınə 'leıbl

embarrassed /ɪm'bærɪst/
expensive /əks'pensɪv/
fashionable /'faʃɪnəbəl/
foreign /'fɒrɪn/
healthy /'helθi/
horrible /'hɒrɪbəl/
incredible /ɪn'kredəbəl/
intelligent /ɪn'telədʒənt/
loose /lu:s/
lucky /'lʌki/
magic /'mædʒiʁ/
necessary /'nesəsəri/
neutral /'nju:trəl/
old-fashioned /əʊld 'fæʃnd/
original /ə'rɪdʒɪnəl/
out of the ordinary
/aʊt əv ðə 'ɔ:dnri/
painful /'peɪnfəl/
patterned /'pætənd/
pierced /'pɪəst/
plain /pleɪn/
really good /reɪli 'gu:d/
relaxed /rə'lækst/
religious /rɪ'lɪdʒəs/
scruffy /'skrʌfi/
smart /smɑ:(r)t/
soft /sɒft/
stylish /'staɪlɪʃ/
tight /taɪt/
trendy /'trendi/
uncomfortable /ən'kʌmftəbəl/
unfashionable /ʌn'fæʃnəbl/
wrong /rɔ:ŋ/

Unit 5

5.1 Adjectives describing art

beautiful /'bju:tɪfʊl/
contemporary /kən'temprəri/
depressing /di'presɪŋ/
expressive /ɪk'spresɪv/
realistic /riə'lɪstɪk/
shocking /'ʃɒkɪŋ/
simple /'sɪmpl/
sophisticated /sə'fɪstɪkeɪtɪd/

5.2 Art: Nouns

abstract /'æbstrækt/
exhibition /eksɪ'bɪʃn/
gallery /'gæləri/
landscape /'lændskeɪp/
mural /'mju:rəl/
nude /nju:d/
portrait /'pɔ:treɪt/
sculpture /'skʌlptʃə(r)/
still life /stɪl laɪf/

5.3 Nouns

advertising agency
/'ædvətaɪzɪŋ eɪdʒənsi/
argument /'ɑ:(r)gjʊmənt/
attempt /ə'tempt/
attendant /ə'tendənt/
attic /'ætɪk/
beauty /'bjʊti/
biography /baɪ'jɒgrəfi/
cleaner /'kli:nə(r)/
climbing equipment
/'klaɪmɪŋ ek'wɪpmənt/
clue /klu:/
collector /kə'lektə(r)/
council /'kaʊnsəl/
critic /'krɪtɪk/
district /'dɪstrɪkt/
emotion /e'məʊʃən/
equipment /ek'wɪpmənt/
expert criminal
/'ekspɜ(r)t 'krɪmɪnəl/
furniture /fɜ:(r)nɪtjə(r)/
graffiti /grə'fi:ti/
health problem /'helθ prɒbləm/
hospital /'hɒspɪtəl/
line /laɪn/
masterpiece /'mɑ:stəpi:s/
materials /mə'tiəriəlz/
meaning /'mi:nɪŋ/
metal /'metəl/
neighbour /'neɪbə(r)/
neighbourhood /'neɪbəhʊd/
operation /ɒpə'reɪʃən/
paint /peɪnt/
painter /'peɪntə(r)/
painting /'peɪntɪŋ/
police /pə'li:s/
prison /'prɪzən/
project /'prəʊdʒekt/
public /'pʌblɪk/
reaction /ri'ækʃn/
risk /rɪsk/
scene /si:n/
shark /ʃɑ:(r)k/
snob /snob/
soup can /'sʊp kæn/
studio /'stju:diəʊ/
style /staɪl/
subject /'sʌbdʒekt/
technique /tek'ni:k/
thief /θi:f/
vandalism /'vændəlɪsəm/
volunteer /vɒlən'tɪə(r)/
walkie-talkie /wɔ:ki 'tɔ:ki/
window /'wɪndəʊ/

5.4 Verbs

arrest /ə'rest/
assassinate /ə'sæsɪneɪt/
break /breɪk/
clean /kli:n/
commit /kəmɪt/
cut off /kʌt 'ɔ:f/
express /əks'pres/
ignore /ɪgnɔ:(r)/
investigate /ɪn'vestəgeɪt/
jump /dʒʌmp/
mark /mɑ:k/
offend /ə'fend/
provoke /prə'vəʊk/
recover /rə'kʌə(r)/
shoot /ʃu:t/
steal /sti:l/

5.5 Other adjectives

artistic /ɑ:(r)'tɪstək/
best /best/
cinematic /sɪnə'mætɪk/
clean /kli:n/
famous /'feɪməs/
inexperienced /ɪnəks'pɪəri:ənsd/
mysterious /mɪ'stirijəs/
physical /'fɪsɪkəl/
positive /'pɒzɪtɪv/
protective /prə'tektɪv/
religious /rɪ'lɪdʒəs/
similar /'sɪmɪlə(r)/
straight /streɪt/
terrible /'terɪbəl/
ugly /'ʌgli/
worried /'wvri:d/

Unit 6

6.1 Body language

bite your nails /baɪt jə 'neɪlz/
blush /blʌʃ/
cry /kraɪ/
hug /hʌg/
point /pɔɪnt/
shake hands /ʃeɪk 'hændz/
smile /smaɪl/
sneer /snɜ:(r)/
stare /steə(r)/

6.2 Adjectives describing character

aggressive /ə'gresiv/
balanced /'bælənst/
cold-blooded /kəʊld'blʌdɪd/
dishonest /dɪs'ɒnɪst/
emotionless /ɪ 'məʊʃnləs/
hot-blooded /hɒt'blʌdɪd/

honest /'ɒnəst/
jealous /'dʒeləs/
kind /kaɪnd/
modest /'mɒdɪst/
moody /'mu:di/
patient /'peɪʃnt/
rude /ru:d/
sensitive /'sensətɪv/
violent /'vaɪələnt/

6.3 Nouns
affection /ə'fekʃən/
anger /'æŋgə(r)/
behaviour /bɪ'heɪvjə(r)/
call /kɔ:l/
chance /tʃɑ:ns/
communication /kəmjʊnɪ'keɪʃən/
eye contact /'aɪ kɒntækt/
gesture /'dʒestʃə(r)/
intruder /ɪn'tru:də(r)/
jealousy /'dʒeləsi/
mate /meɪt/
palm /pɑ:m/
racism /'reɪsɪzəm/
the rest /ðə 'rest/
stranger /'streɪnʒə(r)/
survival /sə(r)'vaɪvəl/
weapon /'wepən/

6.4 Verbs
chew /tʃu:/
communicate /kəm'jʊ:nɪkeɪt/
confess /kən'fes/
criticize /'krɪtɪsaɪz/
cross /krɒs/
drive you mad /draɪv jə 'mæd/
hibernate /'haɪbəneɪt/
jog /dʒɒg/
mimic /'mɪmɪk/
mind /maɪnd/
raise /reɪz/
scare /skeɪ(r)/
tell the truth /tel ðə 'tru:θ/
tidy up /'taɪdijʌp/

6.5 Other adjectives
addictive /ə'dɪktɪv/
basic /'beɪsɪk/
constructive /kən'strʌktɪv/
defensive /dɪ'fensɪv/
male /meɪl/
natural /'nætʃjʊrəl/
obvious /'ɒbviəs/
raw /rɔ:/

6.6 Adverbs
definitely /'defɪnətli/
non-stop /nɒn'stɒp/

Unit 7

7.1 Geographical features
border /'bɔ:də(r)/
continent /'kɒntɪnənt/
desert /'dezət/
equator /ɪ'kweɪtə(r)/
forest /'fɒrɪst/
island /'aɪlənd/
lake /leɪk/
mountain range /'maʊntɪn reɪndʒ/
ocean /'əʊʃən/
pole /pəʊl/

7.2 Other nouns
bandit /'bændɪt/
bungee jumping /'bʌndʒi dʒʌmpɪŋ/
camel /'kæml/
capsule /kæpsju:l/
companion /kəm'pænjən/
cruise /kru:z/
distance /'dɪstəns/
diver /'daɪvə(r)/
expedition /ekspə'diʃən/
extrovert /'ekstrəvɜ:(r)t/
journey /'dʒɜ:(r)ni/
land /lænd/
lift /lɪft/
lodge /lɒdʒ/
monkey /'mʌnki/
mule /mju:l/
nightclubbing /'naɪtklʌbɪŋ/
opportunity /ɒpə(r)'tju:nɪti/
plane /pleɪn/
safari /sə'fɑ:ri/
scorpion /'skɔ:piən/
service /'sɜ:(r)vɪs/
sightseeing /'saɪtsi:jɪŋ/
space /speɪs/
step /step/
tour /tʊə(r)/
tourist /tʊərɪst/
tragedy /'trædʒədi/
trek /trek/
triumph /'traɪʌmf/
wagon /'wægən/
voyage /'vɔɪjɪdʒ/
yacht /jɔ:t/

7.3 Places
Afghanistan /əf 'gænɪstæn/
Asia /'eɪʒə/
Australia /ɒ'streɪlijə/
Egypt /'ɪ:dʒɪpt/
England /'ɪŋglənd/
India /'ɪndjiə/
Iran /ɪ'ræn/
Malta /'mɔ:ltə/
Minnesota /mɪnɪ'səʊtə/
Paris /'pærɪs/
Portugal /'pɔ:(r)tjʊgəl/
Scotland /'skɒtlənd/
The Alps /ðɪ j'ælps/
The Amazon /ðɪ j'æməzɪn
The Atlantic /ðɪ jət'læntɪk/
The Equator /ðɪ jɪk'weɪtə(r)/
The Himalayas /ðə hɪmə'leɪjəz/
The Indian Ocean /ðɪ jɪndijən 'əʊʃən/
The Mediterranean Sea /ðə medɪtə'reɪnijən 'si:/
The Pacific /ðə pə'sɪfɪk/
The River Nile /ðə rɪvə(r) 'naɪl/
The Sahara /ðə sə'hæræ/
The USA /ðə ju: es 'eɪ/
Turkey /'tɜ:(r)ki/
Wales /weɪlz/
Warsaw /'wɔ:(r)sɔ:/

7.4 Verbs
accompany /ə'kʌmpəni/
cheat /tʃi:t/
get on your nerves /get ɒn jə 'nɜ:vz/
go camping /gəʊ 'kæmpɪŋ/
melt /melt/
snore /snɔ:(r)/

Unit 8

8.1 TV programmes
cartoon /kɑ:'tu:n/
chat show /'tʃæt ʃəʊ/
comedy /'kɒmədi/
documentary /dɒkju'mentri/
drama series /'drɑ:mə sɪərɪz/
game show /'geɪm ʃəʊ/
music programme /'mju:zɪk prəʊ græm/
soap opera /'səʊp ɒprə/
sports programme /'spɔ:ts prəʊgræm/
the news /ðə 'nju:z/
the weather /ðe 'weðə(r)/

8.2 Human achievement: verbs and nouns
compete /kəm'pi:t/
competition /kɒmpə'tɪʃn/
competitor /kəm'petɪtə(r)/
compose /kəm'pəʊz/
composer /kəm'pəʊzə(r)/
composition /kɒmpə'zɪʃn/
entertain /entə'teɪn/